Praise for... Black Sheep

'Richard Stephens demonstrates that the bad ("NEVER DO THAT!") things in life do have their good, practical side.'

Marc Abrahams, founder of the Ig Nobel Prize

'Packed with anecdotes from popular culture as well as intriguing accounts of scientific research, this book is a genial and knowledge-able guide to everyday vices from alcohol to chewing gum, which finds that there are often hidden virtues to be found in them, too. Richard Stephens wears his authority as a psychologist lightly, and in a warm, entertaining style offers his perspective that risk is not the same as danger; that life can be enriched by taking a few risks – depending on the context, of course.'

Michael Regnier, Science Writer/Editor
at the Wellcome Trust

Black Sheep

The Hidden Benefits of Being Bad

RICHARD STEPHENS

Black Sheep

The Hidden Benefits of Being Bad

RICHARD STEPHENS

First published in Great Britain in 2015 by Hodder & Stoughton.
An Hachette UK company.
Copyright © Richard Stephens 2015
The right of Richard Stephens to be identified as the Author of the Work has been asserted
by him in accordance with the Copyright, Designs and Patents Act 1988.
Database right Hodder & Stoughton (makers)
British Library Cataloguing in Publication Data: a catalogue record for this title is available
from the British Library.
Library of Congress Catalog Card Number: on file
Paperback ISBN 978 1 47361 081 1
eBook ISBN 978 1 47361 082 8/978 1 47361 083 5
1
The publisher has used its best endeavours to ensure that any website addresses referred to
in this book are correct and active at the time of going to press. However, the publisher and
the author have no responsibility for the websites and can make no guarantee that a site
will remain live or that the content will remain relevant, decent or appropriate.
The publisher has made every effort to mark as such all words which it believes to be
trademarks. The publisher should also like to make it clear that the presence of a word in
the book, whether marked or unmarked, in no way affects its legal status as a trademark.
Every reasonable effort has been made by the publisher to trace the copyright holders
of material in this book. Any errors or omissions should be notified in writing to the
publisher, who will endeavour to rectify the situation for any reprints and future editions.
Typeset by Cenveo® Publisher Services.
Printed and bound in Great Britain by CPI Group (UK) Ltd., Croydon CR0 4YY
John Murray Learning policy is to use papers that are natural, renewable and recyclable
products and made from wood grown in sustainable forests. The logging and manufacturing
processes are expected to conform to the environmental regulations of the country
of origin.
Hodder & Stoughton Ltd
Carmelite House
50 Victoria Embankment
London EC4Y 0DZ
www.hodder.co.uk

Also available
as an ebook

Dedication

This book is dedicated with much love to Mum and Dad, Bette and Alan; to my wife, Maria; and especially to the younger generation of our family, Jenna, Lawren, Leoni, Abigail and, latest addition, Noah.

Acknowledgements

Thanks go to Maria J. Grant, Jamie Joseph, Nicola Jones, Iain Campbell and Martin Frischer for helping in various ways with developing the ideas in this book. Thanks also to Marc Abrahams, James Hartley and Michael Murray for offering advice and encouragement along the way. Thanks also to Alison Pickering for fast and efficient editorial services. I'd like to thank my daughter's primary school teacher, Mr Bullivant, for the science as 'fair test' concept. Last but not least, my sincere thanks to current and former students at Keele University, in part for their energy and enthusiasm, but also for keeping me in touch with the ever-changing landscape of psychology research.

Contents

List of illustrations

Foreword

I know a man who gave up smoking, drinking, sex, and rich food.
He was healthy right up to the day he killed himself.

*Johnny Carson: television host, comedian, writer, producer,
actor and musician.*

In this Age of Information we are constantly inundated with facts, figures and opinions. Eat this, don't eat that; do this, don't do that. The flow of information is relentless. Through all of this a narrative has emerged on what we should be doing to stay healthy – don't drink alcohol, avoid fatty food, take regular exercise. In fact the message seems to be that, if at all possible, we should avoid risk of any kind. But where's the fun in that? Whoever wrote a book or made a film about characters that refused to take a chance?

As human beings we need to take risks to remind ourselves that we are alive. Of course, the trick is to take only the kinds of risks that will be to our ultimate benefit rather than ones that are likely to kill us. Risk-taking is often looked upon as irresponsible and bad – but there are hidden benefits of being bad, not just for the individual transgressor but also more widely. I can say this with some confidence because I am basing it on science – science such as this:

In the early 1980s a very unusual lecture took place. A professor took a risk and consequently what might have been a run-of-the-mill conference presentation instead became unique and memorable. The title of the lecture, 'Vaso-active therapy for erectile dysfunction' was not unusual for the American Urological Society annual meeting. But as his talk got under way some audience members wondered about the unusually informal attire the distinguished academic presenter had chosen to wear that evening. Around midway through, however, all became clear. To gasps, the ageing and bespectacled professor stepped out from behind the rostrum and pulled his tracksuit trousers tightly around his crotch. This act revealed two things to the shrieking and incredulous audience. The first was that the speaker had chosen his own penis as the subject of investigation. The second was that he seemed to be making very good progress with the research...

Picture now a different scene. It's early spring and the head professor of a university psychology department is ambling along its corridors. There is a buzz of activity as undergraduate students conduct the research that they will write up into their final year dissertation reports. From behind ajar doors the professor hears the murmur of answered questions, the click of keyboards and even the sound of music as enthusiastic students put their assumptions and hypotheses to the test. However, the sounds emanating from one doorway stand out, and the professor stops dead trying to fathom out what is occurring as a clear but strained voice repeats a syllable notable for its unexpectedness within the hallowed corridors of a university: 'fuck... fuck... fuck...'. I'll have to confess, that's my lab and those are some of my students carrying out research into the hidden benefits of swearing – finding, in this instance, that bad language can make us more tolerant of pain.

Now imagine you are driving a car. It's a nice day, there are some other vehicles around but it's not congested and you're making good progress. As you pass under one of many bridges across the road I want you to freeze the action and survey the scene in front of you – the view under the bridge, the windscreen, the inside of the car, your own body. Now – what are you doing with your hands? Do you have both hands on the wheel? Maybe one hand is on the gear stick or draped out of the open window. Psychologists from the University of Canterbury, New Zealand, have watched many cars pass under similar bridges and they can tell what kind of driver you are and how likely you are to have an accident based on the very simple matter of how you hold your steering wheel. Clearly it's bad to drive one-handed but psychologists have found one hidden benefit – the very simple matter of how you hold your steering wheel can signal how likely you are to have an accident.

As well as providing scientific insights into the hidden benefits of being bad, the preceding paragraphs provide some examples of what psychology researchers do. At the time of writing, the American Psychological Association's PsycINFO® database contained details of more than three million psychology research papers published worldwide. The topics researched range from social ostracism to emotional intelligence, from music appreciation to pain perception, from religion to death. They are a microcosm of human experience and reflect how the psychology researcher's world is as diverse as the real world it seeks to understand. Through its research psychology has attempted to answer a huge variety of questions around people. It has something to say about sex (What underlies physical attraction?), addiction (Why do some people develop problem drinking?) and bad language (Does swearing serve any purpose?), to name but a few areas. Whatever turns you on, for any human sphere of activity, there's likely to be a piece of psychology research that can inform that interest.

This book is full of the most surprising tales from the world of psychological science illustrating the hidden benefits of being bad. I have done my utmost to portray the science in this book accurately, but there are some caveats to that. In places I have simplified the description of studies so that instead of discussing them in their full intricate detail I have talked only about parts that are relevant. This I have done for the sole purpose of making the science more easily explained and understood by the reader. What I haven't done is made exhaustive searches through entire literatures for all studies that exist on any one topic. It can happen that a study gets published showing X to be the case, but follow-up studies cannot reproduce the effect. It happens – science is full of contradictions and psychological science is no exception. I talk about a number of these (for example contradictory research on whether chewing gum can relieve stress in Chapter 7). However, as a popular science book aiming to tell some interesting stories about research, I may have missed others. Don't take the accounts in these pages as gospel.

People often share opinions on politics, music and sport but rarely on science. Yet there are now cultural movements aiming to bring science into the mainstream and so increase the general level of 'science savvy' in modern life. Examples of these include TV shows such as *Mythbusters* and *Dara Ó Briain's Science Club*, and live evening events such as Cafe Scientifique and Skeptics in the Pub. I think one issue here is a problem with the public perception of what science is. The general view is that science is all about lab coats, high-tech gadgets and indecipherable equations. But that's not the core of what science is – it's actually very simple. When scientists carry out experiments they are looking to set up a fair test of a phenomenon at question – no more or less than this.

I sincerely hope I can convince you of this as you read on and I hope too that I can pique your interest to find out more about psychology research. This is a book about sex, addiction, bad language and fast driving. It tells of the hidden benefits of diverse activities from doodling to chewing gum and from using a footbridge to riding on a roller-coaster. There will be romance, adventure, close brushes with death and an abundance of interesting ideas and fascinating research findings, many of which you won't see coming. Here is an open door into psychological science; why don't you come in?

Richard Stephens
February 2015

I
Sleep around

It was early evening at the 1983 American Urological Society annual meeting in Las Vegas and the scientists and their partners in the audience had already donned dinner jackets and ball gowns in readiness for the conference dinner. The final lecture of the day, 'Vaso-active therapy for erectile dysfunction', would explain a new treatment for impotence involving injecting a drug directly into the penis. However, as Laurence Klotz, who attended the lecture and produced a memoir for posterity, noted, the mode of presentation for conveying the research findings was unique and memorable [*see* Klotz, below].

As the talk got underway some audience members reflected that the speaker, Professor G. S. Brindley of the Institute of Psychiatry, King's College London, was not noted for the unusually informal attire he had chosen to wear that evening. However, they quickly forgot about this as a series of highly explicit slides was projected onto the auditorium screen. The quantity and quality of the erections depicted were beyond dispute but, still, anyone with a healthy scientific scepticism would have been quick to point out that pictures don't prove much on their own. This same thought seemed to be troubling the speaker and this led him to put an odd question to his audience: 'Would a normal person experience sexual arousal as a result of giving a lecture?' Encouraged by shakes of the head, the meeting headed into uncharted waters when Professor Brindley announced that he had injected his own penis shortly before the talk.

The audience had barely processed this shocking revelation when the ageing and bespectacled professor stepped out from behind the rostrum, and to gasps pulled his tracksuit trousers tightly around his crotch. It's difficult to know whether what came next was brave or foolhardy. Still unsatisfied with the demonstration, Brindley took the unprecedented step of dropping his trousers and underwear, the better to display the undoubtedly impressive results of his research. The screams of the female audience members had not yet fully subsided when he set off towards the front row, trousers around ankles, offering the gallery a personal opportunity to 'confirm the degree of tumescence'. However, the hubbub had by now grown so tumultuous that, still some way off, he at last had a change of heart. He pulled up his pants, returned to the rostrum and rapidly brought the talk to a close – but history had been made. Today Giles Brindley's *Wikipedia* page records how, despite accomplishments in a diverse array of scientific fields, he remains best known for this most unusual and memorable conference presentation.

But why should such a hysterical reaction have occurred? It's because sexual activity, in its many different forms, has been frowned upon by societies since Biblical times. As an example, Genesis 38:9 states: 'And Onan knew that the seed should not be his; and it came to pass, when he went in unto his brother's wife, that he spilled it on the ground, lest that he should give seed to his brother. And the thing that he did displeased the Lord: wherefore he slew him also.'

This passage describes Onan's efforts to avoid impregnating his sister-in-law. It gave rise to the word 'onanism', meaning masturbation, and this Biblical passage is widely interpreted as outlawing this sexual practice. The passage highlights the attitude of the Bible towards sexual activity as bad.

However, times change and attitudes towards sex loosened up during the counter-cultural revolution of the 1960s. This all-encompassing movement ushered into the public consciousness new tastes in music, wider acceptance of recreational drug use, the radical politics of feminism, free speech and civil rights, a growing sympathy for revolutionary and anti-war sentiment and a sexual revolution espousing sex before marriage and gay liberation. Today, sexual content has become part of mainstream culture, and yet, in the second decade of the 21st century, sex is still a subject that can provoke discomfort when brought up in public. If you doubt that, picture yourself growing up watching a film on TV with your parents – and remember the mutual, intergenerational, toe-curling awkwardness engulfing the room during a sex scene. Topics related to sex have enormous potential to embarrass – as one scientist, who probably should have known better, found out.

The Brindley episode illustrates much, not least that science is not immune from the taboos and politics of the times. Still, as the barriers to studying sex have come down, including the legalization of certain sex acts that were outlawed not so long ago, there is now a thriving interest in the science of sex. It began with the work of pioneers like the biologist Alfred Kinsey in the 1940s, whose surveys revealed controversially high prevalence in middle class America of taboo sexual practices such as masturbation and oral sex. Then there was the US-based physician and psychologist team of Masters and Johnson in the 1960s, who for the first time observed and measured, up close and personal, human sexual activity in their laboratory.

The scope of studies conducted today span from volunteers viewing erotic material to having them perform live sex acts. Research participants have undergone brain scans, psychological testing and more besides both during and after sex. This means that we are now in a position to know, scientifically, more about the benefits and otherwise of sexual activity in its many forms than ever before. And I don't mean the self-evident reproductive benefits of sex. There are many useful (and some not so useful) side effects of entering a state of sexual arousal. Let's begin with a simple question – have you ever wondered what goes on in your brain during sex?

New uses for old equipment

Researchers at Stanford University in California wanted to find out how sexual arousal activates different parts of the brain [*see* Arnow et al, below]. They did this in a very straightforward way – they had some young men watch erotic movies while undergoing a **functional magnetic imaging** brain scan. Magnetic resonance imaging uses magnetization of atoms in the body to create images of internal organs. Functional magnetic resonance imaging, or **fMRI** for short, is a further refinement that uses the level of blood oxygen to detect changing activity in cells. An fMRI brain scan shows the parts of the brain that become active as people perform different tasks and activities.

The erotic films used in the study depicted couples engaged in intercourse and fellatio. The researchers were unsure whether to show several short two-minute erotic films or a longer nine-minute movie, so they tried both. As it turned out they need not have been overly concerned because sexual arousal was sustained for the duration of both lengths of film. Sports films were also used as a point of comparison. These portrayed sequences of play from American football and baseball games.

Ingeniously, an electrical expanding cuff designed to measure blood pressure was adapted to be placed over the penis to provide an objective measure of each young man's level of 'physiological interest' in the movies. The technical term of this type of interest is **penile turgidity**. My inner science geek loves that there is a correct scientific term for penile erections and that these can be measured and scored such that the more prominent the erection, the greater the turgidity score. I've included a graph from the paper showing how turgidity increased each time a new erotic film started (this is the line of the graph that looks like a mountain range). While the young men were inside the scanner watching the films they were also invited to press a button whenever they found a scene particularly arousing – these button presses are also shown in the graph (marked 'A', 'B' and 'C') and you can see that they mostly correspond with moments of physiological arousal.

So what happens in the sexually aroused brain? The brain regions that became active during the sexual arousal brought about by watching an erotic film were the **visual areas**; the **anterior cingulate gyrus**, which is known to become active as we direct our attention to particular parts of our surroundings; the **hypothalamus**, which is known to coordinate body temperature, hunger, thirst, fatigue and sleep; and structures called the **caudate nucleus** and **insula**, known to be activated as part of the brain's reward pathways. These latter are interesting because they became active for both the erotic movies and the sports movies – but that doesn't mean that men get off on sport. It is well established that the brain has a 'reward circuit' that can be activated by many stimuli.

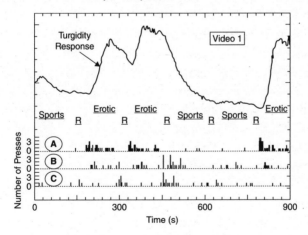

FIGURE 1.1 Experiments on penile turgidity

By permission of Oxford University Press © 'Brain activation and sexual arousal in healthy, heterosexual males' by Arnow, B. A. et al, *Brain*, Vol. 25 pp 1014–23

The caudate nucleus is known to be part of the reward circuit because of research showing that it becomes active in anticipation of receiving money. The insula is known to be part of the reward circuit because it has been shown to become active after taking cocaine. Other brain structures within the reward circuit are the **anterior cingulate** and the **putamen**. These brain structures were shown to become active in a study by researchers from Glasgow University [*see* McLean et al, below] in which male Scottish football fans watched video clips of their team scoring goals (compared with watching clips of near misses or midfield play). The activation of these general reward areas by a wide range of stimuli including watching erotic movies illustrates something very obvious – that sexual arousal is intrinsically rewarding. Here, we have an example of science backing up what everyone already knew – that sex is fun.

Indeed the author Charles Bukowski likened having sex to 'kicking death in the ass while singing'. Clearly there's a big difference between sexual arousal from watching an erotic film and the hugely immersive experience of having sex with another person. Is what happens to the brain during actual sex the same as for sexual arousal? And what about differences between men and women? For example (and as we shall see later on) when it comes to sex, men are thought to be more visually oriented, whereas women are more tactile. Believe it or not some Dutch neuroscientists have carried out a study in which men and women agreed to undergo brain scans while at the same time having sex.

Feel like a man/woman

Researchers from Groningen University in the Netherlands [*see* Georgiadis et al, below] invited couples to perform sexual acts while one of them underwent a brain scan using **Positron**

Emission Tomography (PET). This type of scan involves injecting a radioactive tracer into the blood stream of the person being scanned, and this tracer is what shows up in the images generated by the machine. The areas of the brain that show increased blood flow at a given moment are thought to be working harder, and so to be particularly involved in whatever activity is happening in that moment.

The member of the couple that was being scanned definitely got the better deal. They sat on a comfortable chair, closed their eyes and enjoyed the sexual attention of their partner. The partner had to work a little harder, stimulating the genital area of their mate (penis for males; clitoris for females) sufficiently so that they would reach a state of sustained sexual arousal and eventually orgasm. To reduce unwanted effects the couples were asked not to communicate verbally during the scans. Despite these constraints, and the fact that these couples were having sex under some most unusual conditions, there was sufficient familiarity for the volunteers to agree that there were no important differences between their sexual experience in the scanner and how they usually went about things. Of interest were the similarities and differences in men's and women's brain activity during physical sexual arousal and orgasm.

There were various differences in the brains of people having sex compared with those in the previous study that watched erotic movies. The most apparent gender differences were pre-orgasm. At this point men showed increased activation of the **right posterior claustrum** compared with women. This region of the brain is used for integrating different sense modalities (e.g. touch and vision) and its activation provides one example of how men's sexuality is more visual than that of women. On the other hand, women showed increased activation of the rear part of the **left parietal cortex**, which is a key interface between sensory and motor areas, as well as the motor cortices of the frontal lobes. This difference in men and women might be explained by '**mirror neuron theory**', which is the idea that some parts of the brain connected with muscular movement don't just become active when making movements, but also indirectly from watching another person perform a movement. This indirect activation is likened to a mirroring effect. The finding that women's motor cortices become active when their partner performed genital stimulation on them hints at the idea that women have a higher capacity for sensing the perspective of others than men do. The women seemed to have been mirroring their partner's movements at a neural level.

But the differences between men's and women's brains during sexual arousal are not what interest me most about this paper. What fascinates me is the similarity during orgasm. Men and women showed a clear deactivation of the **orbitofrontal cortex** during the moments of orgasm. This part of the brain, when active, is involved in urge suppression, appetite, self-monitoring and self-referential thought. Deactivation of the orbitofrontal cortex leads to opposite states – respectively, inability to suppress urges, no longer having an appetite (feeling satiated) and an absence of self-monitoring and self-referential thought such as would be associated with a more carefree state of mind.

Men's and women's perspectives on the world can seem so different. How men and women read situations can vary greatly and is captured succinctly by the well-known title of relationship counsellor John Gray's book: *Men Are from Mars, Women Are from Venus*. Can a man ever know what it is like to be a woman? Can a woman understand what it is like to inhabit a man's body? Usually, the answer is that they cannot but perhaps there are certain moments when they come close. The feeling of orgasm is very similar for both sexes to the extent that health professionals (gynaecologists, medics and psychologists) have been unable to tell apart men's and women's verbal descriptions of it. It could just be that the shared deactivated orgasmic brain state may be one instance when the inner workings of the minds of men and women are similar. A hidden benefit of sex is to unite men and women in the mental experience of orgasm – which appears to be identical for males and females. The moment of sexual climax may be when we are mentally closest to the opposite sex.

But as well as this psychological benefit of the act of sex, other more physical benefits can arise from our performances in the bedroom.

Frowns, scowls and grimaces

Beauty therapists like Eva Fraser recommend that you regularly exercise your face to maintain firm and healthy facial muscles. She claims that the muscles of the face can be toned like any other muscles in the body resulting in reduced lines and wrinkles, fuller uplifted cheeks, a firmer jaw line and stronger and lifted eyelids. All this adds up to a younger, healthier appearance, which is very desirable – but is it true? If popularity is any measure of success, then the answer is yes, because her book, Eva Fraser's *Facial Workout* has been in print for more than 20 years. Peering inside, it recommends the reader to undertake ten minutes of various eyebrow-lifting, chin-gurning exercises each day. Now, personally, this is not something that I could commit to – repetitive exercises of any kind are just not my thing. But seeing this book made me wonder whether there might be another more fun way to work out those cheek muscles.

Psychologists have been interested in facial expressions during sex since the pioneering studies of Masters and Johnson who, as I mentioned earlier, spent the 1960s directly observing the sexual encounters of hundreds of couples. Thanks to their observations we know there are four phases of sexual response: the period over which sexual arousal first begins and then steadily increases (the *excitement phase*); a period of heightened arousal immediately before the orgasm arrives (the *plateau phase*); the climax (the *orgasm phase*); and the post orgasm period of relaxation and reorientation to one's surroundings (the *resolution phase*).

Something else became apparent as they closely watched couples making love in their laboratory. They couldn't help but notice their volunteers' exaggerated facial expressions, particularly during the plateau and orgasm phases. Most unusually, and in stark contrast to the harmony and ecstasy that characterize the subjective experience of sexual climax, the couples who had agreed to be scrutinized during these most intimate moments were seen to frown, scowl and grimace their way to sexual fulfilment.

Work on facial expressions during sex was updated recently by psychologists from Universidad Autónoma de Madrid [*see* Fernández-Dols et al, below]. They had heard about a website on which users upload self-shot videos of their facial expressions during orgasm, called www.beautifulagony.com. The researchers obtained 100 clips from the website and then they carefully noted the different facial expressions and the stage of sexual response (excitement, plateau, orgasm or resolution) at which they appeared. They found a number of facial movements that commonly occurred during plateau and orgasm, including 'closing of the eyes' (seen in 92 per cent of clips); 'dropping of the jaw' (79 per cent of clips); 'frowning' (64 per cent of clips); and 'parting of the lips' (45 per cent of clips).

Interestingly, the different combinations of these movements tended to be quite varied among the different users who uploaded videos so that the overall facial expression of any one person during sex was quite an individual thing. There were striking similarities between these sexual facial expressions and the facial expressions displayed during pain, particularly tightening or closing the eyes, raising the upper lip, and drop-ping the jaw. Why should we so contort our features in such an ecstatic moment?

Two fascinating alternative explanations were put forward in the paper. One was that the facial expressions serve the pur-pose of regulating an overly intense sensory experience. In other words, during sex and pain we close our eyes as a strategy to reduce the amount of sensory input (cutting off all vision) making the sensory experience more manageable and easier to handle. The other explanation was that, in both cases, the facial movements observed were involuntary and occurred for no other reason than the repeated physical processes of muscle tension and release. This can explain the similarities with facial expressions during sex and pain – the expressions are not expres-sive, in the way a smile would be an expression of happiness, but are accidents brought about by involuntary muscle spasms. The debate was not resolved one way or the other – a clear case of 'more research needed'.

But, thanks to the Internet users who uploaded videos of some very personal moments (and to the psychologists who watched and analysed them), we have a good scientific record of peoples' facial expressions during sex. Whatever the function of these ecstatic frowns, scowls and grimaces, it is undoubtedly true that having sex would make for an excellent facial work-out. A hidden benefit of being bad and sleeping around is exer-cising the facial muscles to help you stay looking young and fit.

And that's not the only physical benefit of a good sexual workout. There is a darker side of sex exemplified by the Mar-quis de Sade and Leopold von Sacher-Masoch, men who practised and wrote novels about, respectively, sexual sadism and masochism. Their writings illustrate that the connection between sex and pain has a long history. But is it true – are sex and pain linked? One line of research shows they are – because during sex we can become more tolerant of pain.

More beautiful agony

Animal behaviour scientists from Rutgers University in New-ark [*see* Whipple & Komisaruk, below] were exploring natural anaesthetics in the animal world that had promise for eventual use in people. They had found that female rats showed fewer pain responses, such as vocalizations or tail flicks, if they were having their vagina stimulated at the same time. On the face of it this seems like rather bizarre research – where might the idea have come from to try this in the first place? Unfortu-nately, the paper doesn't say, however, reducing pain and suf-fering is a noble research agenda so let's assume the researchers were well intentioned. One problem with animal research is that the subjects – the animals – are (of course) unable to give verbal reports. The researchers could not rule out the possibil-ity that vaginal stimulation was itself painful, deflecting other feelings of pain. In order to check for certain whether vagi-nal stimulation eases pain without causing further discomfort there was only one thing for it.

The researchers had some women volunteers undergo a human version of the rat study. The pain perception test-ing procedure made use of a device that applied pressure to a finger using a screw mechanism – a modern day version of the thumbscrew or pillywinks torture instrument of medieval Europe. Of interest were the levels of pressure required to pro-duce pain (known as the pain detection threshold) and, as the screw continued to turn, the amount of pressure that could be withstood before asking for it to cease (known as pain toler-ance). While undergoing these procedures, the women volun-teers consented to stimulate themselves in the most intimate of places using a facial vibrator.

I'll confess I had to use Google to find out what a facial vibrator was. It turns out to be a battery-powered vibrating metal or plastic cylinder designed to stimulate the skin of the face. You would use one of these with the aim of reducing wrinkles and restoring skin firmness and elasticity, although the face is not the only region of the body that can benefit from being touched with one of these devices. The paper doesn't say what arrangements were made for privacy during what was a very intimate procedure, other than the addition of carpets and low-level lighting. It is confirmed that the women volunteers found what they were asked to do not at all stressful.

The researchers found, during vaginal stimulation by means of a vibrator, that the pain detection threshold was increased by 42 per cent and pain tolerance was increased by 30 per cent. Yet touch threshold, ascertained by stroking the back of the hand lightly with a nylon brush, was no different in the vaginal stimulation and control (non-stimulation) conditions. In a second study the women used the vibrator for longer with the aim of inducing an orgasm. Four women reached orgasm and during their moments of climax their pain detection threshold was further increased to 107 per cent above no stimulation, and pain threshold was further increased to 75 per cent above no stimulation. Again, the touch threshold remained unchanged.

The researchers' main question of whether their earlier findings in rats would also apply for people was answered affirmatively. Women felt less pain from a thumbscrew when they touched their vagina with a vibrator, and, of course, the sexual stimulation was not painful in itself. Distraction was ruled out as the main explanation because if the vaginal stimulation were merely distracting then this should have affected sensitivity to being touched, but the women could feel a brush stroking the back of their hand the same as they would normally. There were two reasons put forward in the paper as to why vaginal stimulation would reduce sensitivity to pain. One was that sexual stimulation resulting in extreme pleasure produces a natural analgesia by releasing the neurotransmitters **serotonin** and

norepinephrine. Alternatively, reduced pain sensitivity during vaginal stimulation could be nothing to do with sexual arousal but could instead be related to childbirth, which, like sex, features a good deal of pushing and pulling of the vagina. This ties in with other research showing that women's pain detection thresholds increase during pregnancy. At the moment we don't know whether this theory is right but a very straightforward test of it would be to look at the effects of genital stimulation on men's pain threshold. If the pain reduction effect is related to childbirth then men should not experience it. We await this research being carried out.

We've seen how having sex provides an opportunity for an impromptu facial workout and makes people more able to tolerate pain. But sex is a very physical thing and this level of exertion can take its toll. Some studies done with animals confirm that this is the case – but not always. In fact sometimes the opportunity for sex can push us beyond our usual physical limits. To find out more we need to travel to Australia and meet a very promiscuous but rather bashful species of squid.

Sex, sex and more sex

Having sex uses a lot of energy and it's not surprising that afterwards tiredness and fatigue set in. Researchers from the Zoology Department of the University of Melbourne in Australia have verified this by closely observing the dumpling squid [*see* Franklin et al, below]. They placed live squid in a tube within a water container and watched them swimming against a current. The bottom end of the tube was covered with a mesh and after a while, when the squid became tired, they would stop swimming and come to rest on the mesh. At this point three gentle prods would prompt further swimming. But eventually, even after prodding, the squid were too exhausted to swim any more. Here we have a simple but effective scientific measure of animal behaviour. On average, it took the squid exactly two minutes (120 seconds) to become exhausted from swimming against a current.

For the main experiment, male and female squid were placed together in tanks and usually they would begin copulating within 30 minutes. Apparently, so it says in the paper, the human experimenters watched the mating squid from behind a curtain to avoid disturbing them – I had no idea that squid were shy! Immediately after mating, the squid again underwent the physical challenge of swimming against a current. Now the average time to reach exhaustion was halved to 60 seconds. The squid, worn out by having sex, were much less able to swim against a current. This was a straightforward study doing exactly what it says on the tin (so to speak) but it provides objective, scientific evidence that sex really does sap energy.

FIGURE 1.2 Mating squid

It's true that much can be learned from studying animal behaviour. For example, rats also have been shown to become less active following sex. Although not always. In fact, rat research has revealed that there's a very good way to beat the energy sapping effects of having sex – by having more sex. I'll explain how in a moment but first I have to tell you a story about a US president.

John Calvin Coolidge Jr. was the US president from 1923 to 1929. Coolidge's presidency steered the US through a period of unprecedented economic growth that became known as the roaring twenties. A renowned leader whose reputation has remained strong to this day, one of Coolidge's more obscure legacies was the lending of his name to a psychobiological phenomenon – thanks to a singularly trivial event. The story goes that President Coolidge and his wife were being shown around a farm. They were led around separately, viewing different parts of the farm at different times. At the chicken yard, Mrs Coolidge observed a rooster mating very actively and asked how often this occurred. Surprised to hear it was dozens of times a day she joked that the staff should tell the president when he came by. When the president arrived later, the farm staff duly recounted his wife's observations concerning the rooster. Coolidge responded by asking a simple but revealing question – whether it was the same hen each time. On hearing to the contrary he suggested the staff might like to mention that to Mrs Coolidge.

The Coolidge Effect, named after the 30th president of the United States, is concerned not with industrial relations, economics or outstanding leadership. Rather, it concerns an aspect of sexual behaviour. Specifically, it denotes an observation that holds for many species, that having reached a state of sexual exhaustion, males will become eager to mate once more if a new female becomes available, as opposed to one that is familiar. In technical terms, males have been found to display a shorter refractory period (that is, the time between one copulating session and the next) if a new partner is introduced. The research underlying the Coolidge Effect was written up in the 1960s by scientists from the University of California [*see* Wilson et al, below].

For the main experiment male rats were paired up with females on heat and allowed to mate until they stopped for at least 30 minutes, at which point they were declared to be sexually exhausted. Then the female was removed. Next, some of the males were introduced to a new on-heat female while others were re-introduced to the same on-heat female that they had reached sexual exhaustion with. Sexual activity during the re-introduction phase was recorded, in particular the number of times the female was mounted and the percentage of male rats achieving first and second ejaculations. (How the researchers were able to detect the occurrence of a rat ejaculation I can scarcely imagine, and sadly the paper doesn't explain.)

At first there were no obvious differences with the numbers of mountings and first ejaculations being similar whether or not a new female was reintroduced. However, none of the rats re-introduced to the original partner ejaculated for a second time, whereas several of the rats with new partners did enjoy what might be termed a 'second coming'. In an additional re-introduction phase, when the partner was new 86 per cent of males achieved ejaculation, a much higher proportion than the 33 per cent managing this when the same partner was reintroduced. It works for females too – a paper from the mid-1980s found a Coolidge Effect in female hamsters re-introduced to the same or a new male partner [*see* Lester & Gorzalka, below].

This line of research is still ongoing, but has grown in sophistication. A Mexican team published a Coolidge Effect paper in 2012 that measured sperm count and erection occurrence as well as the number of mounts and ejaculations [*see* Tlachi-López et al, below]. This is great, but I can't help thinking that measuring erection occurrence in rats must be very difficult due to the small size of a rat's penis (sorry rats – no offence intended). Why might the Coolidge Effect exist? It is probably easiest to understand from the perspective of evolution and the need for continuation of a species. The evolutionary advantage of the Coolidge Effect is to encourage a wider circle of copulation partners, so increasing the chances of pregnancy and procreation. Think of it as Nature's way of guarding against putting all your eggs in the same basket, as the old saying goes.

So, sex will make you exhausted but, paradoxically, it can also re-energize you via the Coolidge Effect of the promise of further sex with a new partner. The antidote to sexual exhaustion is more sex!

Staying with rats, a different group of researchers noticed how relaxed their animals appeared following copulation. This made them wonder – could sex also be an antidote to stress?

Sex chills

Researchers from Princeton University in the US encouraged a group of male rats to have sex by placing them with on-heat females [see Leuner et al, below]. After 28 days of this a very neat test of rat anxiety was carried out which anybody with rodents for pets could try out at home. Known technically as the 'the novelty suppressed feeding paradigm', the test very simply involves seeing how long it takes a rat to eat a 2 g food pellet in an unfamiliar, brightly lit open arena. The more anxious the rat, the longer it takes to eat the pellet.

Male rats that had been having regular sex ate their pellets in the open arena relatively quickly. Some other male rats had also been provided with female company but the female was not on heat so for these creatures the relationship was strictly platonic. In the absence of regular sex male rats took, on average, almost twice as long to eat their pellet compared with the males allowed to have regular sex with a receptive female. This is a clear sign that regular sex reduces anxiety.

Research with human volunteers backs this up. A psychologist at the University of Paisley asked a group of male and female adult volunteers to keep a two-week diary of their sexual activity. Following this they were asked to perform a stressful public-speaking task. Those that had had sex, and specifically penile-vaginal intercourse (as opposed to other kinds of partnered sex or masturbation) showed improved blood pressure reactivity and lower stress levels than those that had not [*see* Brody, below]. These studies indicate that a further hidden benefit of regular sex is that it reduces stress. This terribly bad thing called sex seems to be very good for us.

Some of the papers I have been talking about employed 'on-heat' female rats. Oftentimes in the animal world females must be on heat for copulation to take place. 'On heat' simply means the females are at the time in their menstrual cycle when pregnancy is most likely to result from copulation. Women also have a time of the month when fertility is raised, and so the phenomenon of being on heat applies to humans too. How being on heat is signalled between women and men has sparked some fascinating research.

The colour red

Red has long been associated with dominance, something that I know well as a fan of Liverpool Football Club. The club famously switched from red shirts and white shorts to an all red kit in the mid-1960s, heralding a 20-year period of domestic and European dominance unmatched in English football. Manager Bill Shankly said at the time, '...we switched to all red and it was fantastic. The introduction of the all scarlet strip had a huge psychological effect... for the first time there was a glow like a fire was burning'.

And this is not mere hearsay. There is good scientific evidence underlining the advantage in sports conferred by the colour red. Anthropologists from Durham University carried out a study in which they were able to arrange for contestants in combat sports at the 2004 Olympics to wear either red or blue body protectors [see Hill & Barton, below]. They found that there was a small but statistically significant increase in the number of victories for boxers and wrestlers wearing red (55 per cent won their bouts) compared with those in blue (45 per cent won their bouts). Why should this be?

One influential theory as to why red heralds success and dominance is sexual, acknowledging the strong link between red and sexual attraction. The theory holds that women wear artificial red signals, such as red lipstick, because these are perceived by men as an outward sign of female fertility. The specific reason why a woman wearing red lipstick would be attractive to men, according to the theory, is because it signals that her genitalia are of a similar hue, indicating that she is both fertile and sexually receptive. The theory is based on the finding that male rhesus macaques would spend significantly longer looking at images of female macaque genitalia when the images had been digitally manipulated to a deeper shade of red. Also that male chacma baboons would masturbate more frequently when presented with females whose genitalia had been enhanced to appear redder using prosthetics.

It is always tricky to extrapolate research findings from animals to humans. Anthropologists from the University of Kent wondered how safe an assumption it was that these findings with monkeys would still hold in similar experiments carried out with humans [see Johns et al, below]. The researchers set up a fair test of the theory that men, like rhesus macaques, prefer redder female genitalia by showing some young men a series of close up photographs of female genitalia that had been re-coloured into: pale pink, light pink, dark pink or red.

A preference for the red-coloured image would support a sexual origin of the power of the colour red. It is worth mentioning at this juncture the lengths that the researchers went to in order to carry out, with poise and good ethics, what could be perceived as quite a 'dodgy' study.

The images were obtained from a website called www.vul-vavelvet.org. The site was designed to illustrate the variety of shapes of healthy adult female genitalia with the aim of helping women feel comfortable about their bodies. The researchers carefully selected images that were taken from similar angles, did not contain potentially distracting objects (like fingers, sex toys or piercings) and were hairless to account for the current fashion. The images that were used were cropped to remove the **labia minora** (the inner lips of the vagina) and **clitoris**, so that what remained was a view of the lower and left side of the vagina. The researchers gained the permission of the website owner to use the images and they wrote that this permission was an important factor in lending legitimacy to the use of these images for a research study.

When the men viewed and provided ratings for the differently coloured images, their preferences were the opposite to that which would support the sexual origin of the power of the colour red. The participants rated red as the least attractive of the four shades, and they had no preference among the three shades of pink. The amount of sexual experience that each male volunteer had did not have any influence on his vulva colour preferences. What does this mean? The finding that the men were averse to the red vulva image suggests that the potency of the colour red is not connected with sexuality. In fact, this makes sense – it's unlikely that women have ever used their genital skin as a signal to attract males because the two-legged bipedal posture of humans means that the female genitalia are not an easily displayable symbol of sexual receptiveness.

Indeed, the researchers put forward that women's genitalia actually does NOT change colour to any degree. They cited as evidence a previous paper in the *Journal of Sex Research* that analysed *Playboy* magazine centrefolds from 1957–2007. There were no signs that the labia minora varied in colour from woman to woman to any significant degree. It's more likely that a red vulva would be seen as a signal of menstruation. Fertility is at its lowest during the bleeding associated with ovulation making it unlikely that men would be genetically programmed to prefer a red vulva.

And yet there are red lights outside brothels and it has been consistently found that men rate women associated with red objects as more sexually attractive. What can explain the strong links between sex and the colour red? The authors argue that it may be linked to aggression and blood spilled during fighting. Women in red contexts may be rated as more sexually attractive because of an indirect association with male competition rather than because red directly signals sexual fertility or the colour of a woman's genitals.

This chapter has brought to light some of the lesser-known benefits of having sex but there are occasions when sex and sexual arousal can be detrimental. One good, though hackneyed example of this is the idea of a woman using sex to influence a man to do something against his better judgement. Sometimes crudely referred to as 'thinking with the penis', this actually does have a scientific basis.

Just say 'no'

Psychologists from the University of Duisburg-Essen, Germany [*see* Laier et al, below], had some young men perform a sexed-up version of a well-used test of decision-making known as the Iowa Gambling Task. Volunteers pick up cards from among four decks and depending on the card they either receive a small payment or pay a small fine. People usually work out by trial and error which are the advantageous and which are the disadvantageous decks and are able to finish the task making an overall profit rather than a loss. However, in this study the task was adapted by having the plain sides of the cards decorated with photographs. Some of the photographs were sexually explicit (e.g. a couple having vaginal intercourse) and the male heterosexual volunteers taking part were somewhat thrown by them. Instead of the profitable decks the volunteers showed a clear preference for the decks carrying the erotic pictures. The sexually arousing pictures overrode the usual learning-from feedback that takes place in the Iowa Gambling Task. This research shows how decision-making can be impaired by sexual arousal. In fact, this has been a consistent finding in men, although women don't seem to fall for it at all. Or rather, that was thought to be the case, until recently.

A study carried out by some Belgian marketing scientists asked female heterosexual volunteers to rate items of clothing in terms of how soft they felt to the touch and the quality of the fabric [see Festjens et al, below]. Ostensibly they were taking part in some marketing research for a major clothing store, but actually this was a cover story to prevent the women from guessing the real reason why they had been asked to handle the fabrics. After handling and rating the clothes the women were asked to answer the question: 'I am indifferent between receiving 15 Euros now and _____ Euros in one week.' They had to come up with a number to fill in the blank.

This is an example of an impatience discounting task making use of the principal that a bird in the hand is worth two in the bush. In other words, there is a general tendency to prefer immediate gains (holding one bird) over gains in the future (a yet to be caught pair of birds hiding in the bushes). This leads most people to insert a sum greater than 15 Euros in the blank. Importantly, the more impatient one is for the immediate gain, the higher the figure that is given for the future gain (equivalent to valuing a bird in the hand as worth three or perhaps even four in the bush).

But how might the mere act of handling some fabric change how women view a financial transaction? What if I told you that on some occasions the women were asked to handle men's underwear? Handling and rating men's boxer shorts increased the women's impatience such that they asked for an average of 1 extra Euro in a week compared with women who handled t-shirts. The difference rose to 3 Euros when the women were asked to think forward 1 month rather than 1 week. Though relatively small, these increases were statistically significant and they indicate that women, like men, make less advantageous (impatient) decisions in the presence of sexually laden stimuli.

A follow-up study in the same paper had a 'seeing only' condition in which the boxer shorts were behind Plexiglas® and it included some heterosexual male volunteers who handled bras rather than boxer shorts. Another difference is that this time a different valuation task following handling or seeing the garments was used in which the men and women were asked how much they would be willing to pay for luxury items like a bottle of wine and a box of chocolates. It turned out that the women were willing to pay more for luxury items after handling the boxers, but not after seeing them. But the men were willing to pay more after either handling a bra or just seeing a bra.

This verifies what was found in the first study – that women, like men, change how they make decisions in the face of sexually laden stimuli. It also provides another illustration of how men's sexual response can be quite visually based in a way that is not the case for women. Taken together, these findings illustrate that sexual arousal can make men and women more impulsive and as a consequence make decisions that might seem right in the moment, but are actually loss-making over the longer term.

But if sex impairs decision-making what might some of the consequences of that be? A unique Internet survey carried out by psychologists from the University of South Dakota highlighted a serious safety issue when it asked some 700 male and female students about their experiences of sex in moving cars [*see* Struckman-Johnson et al, below]. While the majority of respondents expressed an unfavourable attitude towards sex while driving a moving vehicle, there was a notable sex difference; men rated it as less unfavourably than women did. But the number of people in the survey that admitted having had sex of one kind or another while driving was high, at 33 per cent of the men and 9 per cent of the women. The most frequent sex act was oral sex (78 per cent), which explains how it was that 29 per cent of women and 9 per cent of men admitted to having had sex as a passenger. The most frequent sex acts after oral were genital touching with another (67 per cent), masturbation (14 per cent) and vaginal sex (12 per cent). Some of the consequences that were reported would probably make most people think twice before embarking on sex in a moving vehicle.

Driving mishaps during sex included drifting into another lane, letting go of the steering wheel, speeding and almost hitting another vehicle, pedestrian or object. Personal mishaps included injuring oneself due to features of the vehicle (ouch!), being watched by unwanted passers-by, and being caught by friends, family or the police. This survey illustrates some rather extreme ways in which sexual arousal can upset decision-making – to a life endangering extent. Actually this is similar to the boxer shorts study – people favour the immediate gain of having sex over possible longer term losses such as death, injury or perpetual embarrassment if you happened to get caught!

Emotion in motion

This chapter has highlighted a number of hidden benefits of sex based on evidence from the scientific literature. Who knew that scientists have been having such fun in their laboratories all of this time? We've seen how sexual arousal lights up the brain's reward pathways in the same way as drugs and watching your football team score a goal. This provides a demonstration, if one were needed, that sex is officially fun. We've seen how, at the moment of orgasm, brain activity is very similar in men and women – making a sexual climax a moment when we might most understand what it feels like to be a member of the opposite sex. Sex can provide a facial workout that will keep you looking young, it can be an antidote to pain and anxiety, and while it takes a toll physically, this can be eradicated by the promise of more sex with a novel partner. We've seen that the colour red has a power that confers advantage in sports, but this isn't explained by sex. And sex can be detrimental, impairing the ability of men and women to make decisions, in some cases in quite an extreme fashion.

Mae West once said sex was 'emotion in motion' and it goes without saying that sex is fundamental to being human. While G. S. Brindley's denuded tracksuit exploits were misjudged he is one of many researchers who have had the courage to be unconventional and shed some scientific light on the human sexual response. In so doing these researchers have taught us new things about sex that help us better understand ourselves. Their work is also a wonderful demonstration of the scientific process – encapsulating the fundamentals of scientific reasoning and the design of meaningful experiments and research. Having romped through the world of sex viewed through the lens of science, the next chapter will turn to another 'bad' that is close to many people's hearts.

Further reading

Arnow, B. A., Desmond, J. E., Banner, L. L., Glover, G. H. et al (2002), 'Brain activation and sexual arousal in healthy, heterosexual males', *Brain*, Vol. 125 pp 1014–23

Brody, S. (2006), 'Blood pressure reactivity to stress is better for people who recently had penile-vaginal intercourse than for people who had other or no sexual activity', *Biological Psychology*, Vol. 71 Issue 2 pp 214–22

Fernández-Dols, J-M., Carrera, P. & Crivelli, C. (2011), 'Facial Behavior While Experiencing Sexual Excitement', *Journal of Nonverbal Behavior*, Vol. 35 Issue 1 pp 63–71

Festjens, A., Bruyneel, S. & Dewitte, S. (2014), 'What a feeling! Touching sexually laden stimuli makes women seek rewards', *Journal of Consumer Psychology*, Vol. 24 Issue 3 pp 387–93

Franklin, A. M., Squires, Z. E. & Stuart-Fox, D. (2012), 'The energetic cost of mating in a promiscuous cephalopod', *Biology Letters*, Vol. 8 Issue 5 pp 754–6

Fraser, Eva, *Eva Fraser's facial workout* (Penguin, London, 1992)

Georgiadis, J. R., Reinders, A. A., Paans, A. M., Renken, R. & Kortekaas, R. (2009), 'Men versus women on sexual brain function: prominent differences during tactile genital stimulation, but not during orgasm', *Human Brain Mapping*, Vol. 30 Issue 10 pp 3089–101

Gray, John, *Men Are from Mars, Women Are from Venus* (HarperCollins, New York, 1992)

Hill, R. A. & Barton, R. A. (2005), 'Red enhances human performance in contests', *Nature*, Vol. 435 p 293

Johns, S. E., Hargrave,L. A. & Newton-Fisher, N. E. (2012), 'Red Is Not a Proxy Signal for Female Genitalia in Humans', *PLOS ONE*,Vol. 7 Issue 4

Klotz, L. (2005), 'How (not) to communicate new scientific information: a memoir of the famous Brindley lecture', *BJU International*,Vol. 96 Issue 7 pp 956–7

Laier, C., Pawlikowski, M. & Brand, M. (2014), 'Sexual Picture Processing Interferes with Decision-Making Under Ambiguity', *Archives of Sexual Behavior*, Vol. 43 Issue 3 pp 473–82

Lester, G. L. L. & Gorzalka, B. B. (1988), 'Effect of novel and familiar mating partners on the duration of sexual receptivity in the female hamster', *Behavioral and Neural Biology*, Vol. 49 Issue 3 pp 398–405

Leuner, B., Glasper, E. R.& Gould, E. (2010), 'Sexual Experience Promotes Adult Neurogenesis in the Hippocampus Despite an Initial Elevation in Stress Hormones', *PLOS ONE,* Vol. 5 Issue 7

McLean, J., Brennan, D., Wyper, D., Condon, B., Hadley, D. & Cavanagh, J. (2009), 'Localisation of regions of intense pleasure response evoked by soccer goals', *Psychiatry Research-Neuroimaging*,Vol. 171 Issue 1 pp 33–43

Struckman-Johnson, C., Gaster, S. & Struckman-Johnson, D. (2014), 'A preliminary study of sexual activity as a distraction for young drivers, *Accident Analysis & Prevention*, Vol. 71 pp 120–8

Tlachi-López, J. L., Eguibar, J. R., Fernández-Guasti, A. & Lucio, R. A. (2012), 'Copulation and ejaculation in male rats under sexual satiety and the Coolidge effect', *Physiology & Behavior*,Vol. 106 Issue 5 pp 626–30

Whipple, B. & Komisaruk, B. R. (1985), 'Elevation of pain threshold by vaginal stimulation in women', *Pain*, Vol. 21 Issue 4 pp 357–67

Wilson, J. R., Kuehn, R. E. & Beach, F. A. (1963), 'Modification in the sexual behavior of male rats produced by changing the stimulus female', *Journal of Comparative and Physiological Psychology*, Vol. 56 Issue 3 pp 636–44

Other sources

www.liverpoolecho.co.uk/sport/football/football-news/50-years-on-liverpool-became-8167793
www.beautifulagony.com

2

Drink up

'If when you say whiskey you mean the devil's brew, the poison scourge, the bloody monster, that defiles innocence, dethrones reason, destroys the home, creates misery and poverty, yea, literally takes the bread from the mouths of little children… then certainly I am against it.'

'But, if when you say whiskey you mean the oil of conversation, the philosophic wine, the ale that is consumed when good fellows get together, that puts a song in their hearts and laughter on their lips, and the warm glow of contentment in their eyes… then certainly I am for it.'

Which of these two descriptions would you agree with most? I'm definitely in the songs-in-hearts and laughter-on-lips camp but that reflects my life and my experiences with alcohol, both my own and others' use. To me alcohol represents fun nights out, laughter and silliness. But your experiences might have been very different. Alcohol has a split personality and these two polarized views sum this up very well.

In fact these lines were actually part of the same famous speech delivered in Mississippi in 1952 by Judge Noah S. Sweat, Junior. The US state of Mississippi was particularly oriented towards the temperance movement, operating its own state-wide prohibition of alcohol for over half a century, from 1907 to 1966, which was a good deal longer than the 13-year national US ban lasting from 1920 to 1933. Yet it was a source of considerable annoyance to politicians that while 1950s Mississippi was legally dry, the reality of illegal distilling and underground liquor running meant that alcohol was abundantly available on the black market. Public opinion was split on the matter, from the 'drys', who formed the mainstay of the temperance movement, through to the 'wets', who were the ones buying, drinking and probably in many cases producing alcohol for the black market.

Politicians campaigning and speaking at public meetings knew whatever they said in relation to alcohol would be sure to upset a good proportion of the crowd. So step forward Judge Sweat, who in delivering the 'If by whiskey' speech, invented a perfect 'get-out' for no-win situations like this. His speech gave the appearance of expressing an opinion without actually taking a stand, a strategy known as a **relativist fallacy**. The 'If by whiskey' speech professes a profound commitment to both sides of the argument (from *devil's brew* one moment to *warm glow* the next) with the sole intention of bamboozling the audience – which was achieved to great effect with the final punchline: 'This is my stand. I will not retreat from it. I will not compromise.'

As well as illustrating some cunning political fleet of foot, 'If by whiskey' perfectly sums up the double-think that, to this day, surrounds alcohol and other recreational drugs. We humans have been attracted to alcohol since our ancestors first got drunk eating over-ripe fermenting fruit picked up off the ground. But for as long as alcohol has been brewed, sold and consumed there has been a dark side to its nature – and this negative view of alcohol seems most dominant these days. But not here in *Black Sheep: The Hidden Benefits of Being Bad*. In this chapter I'll be talking about some of the hidden benefits of alcohol and why you certainly wouldn't want to cut it out completely. I'll be explaining why ideas on alcoholism have moved on, the evidence that alcohol can protect against some illnesses, and how it can set the creative juices flowing and lubricate social interaction. Not only that – one of its best features is that for many people it comes with its own 'stop' button.

Returning to the dark days of Prohibition era USA, you would have to say that the decision by one nation to ban alcohol completely was not a great success, providing as it did the backdrop for organized crime, Al Capone and the St Valentine's Day Massacre. If only America had listened to its medical community.

FIGURE 2.1 Scene from *The St Valentine's Day Massacre* (1967) directed by Roger Corman

Doctors versus Prohibition

Alcohol has been a traditional element of a doctor's toolkit since way back. Brandy, known to rapidly increase heart rate and blood pressure, was widely prescribed as a cardiac stimulant in the late 19th century. On the other hand, recognizing its depressant effects, it was also used as a sedative to combat insomnia and reduce breathlessness during fever. This is more evidence of the double-think that surrounds alcohol – reconciling these opposing actions (stimulant v. sedative) caused some difficulties.

Nevertheless, alcohol continued to be widely prescribed into the 20th century. This meant that the introduction of nationwide Prohibition in the US created a face-off between the doctors who wanted to continue prescribing alcohol, and the politicians who were the architects of the ban. A partial peace was achieved with a special dispensation for 'medicinal liquor', but with very strict conditions, including limits on how much could be prescribed and the requirement for a special permit. There still remained, however, the problem that a great many doctors in the US at that time were in the habit of prescribing beer for all manner of illnesses. Beer was not mentioned in the special dispensation.

The doctors were incensed that politicians could meddle in their affairs. Surely after their many hard years of training they knew best what should be prescribed for their patients. So it was that medics formed their own political party, the Medical Rights League, and put forward a candidate for election [*see* Pain, below]. The mainstay of their manifesto was the legalization of medicinally prescribed beer. The group achieved much, not least persuading the American Medical Association to endorse the therapeutic use of alcohol. However, despite this success, the Medical Rights League did not achieve its ultimate aim and beer never was included alongside liquor as being exempt from prohibition for medicinal purposes.

Today, you might think that the idea of any type of alcohol being beneficial for health or wellbeing as pure quackery and a throwback to the bad old days before medical research became prominent. These days it's certainly true that alcohol is viewed by the medical profession as more 'devil's brew' than 'oil of conversation', to use Judge Sweat's terms. But not entirely so. There are many recognized benefits of alcohol and, indeed, some of the harms of alcohol are not so starkly stated as they were even a few years ago. Like the disappearance of the label 'alcoholic' from medical diagnosis, for instance.

No such thing as an alcoholic

The common view of addiction to drugs, including alcohol, is that it is biological. Most people think of addiction in terms of creating chemical changes in the brain – like flicking a biological switch. Once addicted, free will is severely impaired and the user becomes compelled by forces beyond their control to take more and more of the stuff. In the case of drink, they have become an 'alcoholic', or at least 'alcohol dependent'. But what if I told you that, medically, those terms, along with 'alcohol abuse' have fallen out of use?

One of the most authoritative voices defining psychological conditions worldwide is the American Psychiatric Association's *Diagnostic and Statistical Manual of Mental Disorders*, known as DSM for short. The DSM ditched the term alcoholism in its third edition published in the 1980s, instead focusing on 'alcohol dependence' and 'alcohol abuse' [*see* National Institute on Alcohol Abuse and Alcoholism, below]. This reflected a strategic move favouring systematic research findings over the subjective judgement of clinicians. A diagnosis of 'alcohol dependence' was made for symptoms such as being unable to cut down or control alcohol use, drinking more alcohol than intended or showing signs of withdrawal when alcohol is not consumed (such as the 'shakes'), and needing to drink greater and greater quantities to achieve the same subjective feeling of inebriation known as tolerance. A diagnosis of 'alcohol abuse' was made for less severe cases where, nevertheless, alcohol was disrupting family or work responsibilities.

However, in May 2013 when the 5th edition of the DSM was released these terms were not included. They had been replaced by a new single diagnosis of 'alcohol use disorder', which is applied when between 2 and 11 symptoms of problem drinking are present in a 12-month period. The symptoms include craving for alcohol, failure to fulfil major role obligations, tolerance and withdrawal. The 'alcohol use disorder' diagnosis can be mild (2-3 symptoms), moderate (4-5 symptoms) or severe (more than 5 symptoms).

The diagnosis criteria [*see* NIH, below] were changed because medical staff treating people with drinking issues had come to the conclusion that classifying people as *either* abusing alcohol *or* being dependent on it was rather arbitrary [*see* Grohol, below]. The people they were seeing in their clinics had varying degrees of the same problem. Rather than the lesser category of abuse and the more severe category of dependence, now the diagnosis depends on how many symptoms are present. Now, I'm not trying to downplay the seriousness that alcohol use disorder can wreak on people's lives. But why would the American Psychiatric Association abandon the term alcoholism, something that on the face of it seems quite straightforward? One reason is because addiction – even heroin addiction – is not the simple biological process that most people think. A really neat bit of science demonstrating this was the famous 'Rat Park' study by Bruce K. Alexander and colleagues from Simon Fraser University in Canada in the 1970s [*see* Alexander below].

Most luxurious housing for rats

A supposedly scientific basis for drug addiction was established in the 1950s and 1960s when it was repeatedly found that laboratory rats given the choice between the naturally occurring opiate from which heroin is derived, morphine, or clean water, will more often choose morphine. However, nobody had thought to investigate whether the **environmental conditions** in which these experiments took place might have any bearing on the results. Yet, they should have suspected that this may have been important for reasons that even a child would know. Why do rats make good pets?

According to the RSPCA website, rats are intelligent, highly social animals with an excellent sense of touch and a wonderful sense of smell. They are incredibly rewarding animals to look after and pet rats can form close human-animal bonds with their carers. These gregarious, wide-ranging and curious creatures would find it very unpleasant to be shut away in the small solitary cages routinely employed in science laboratories. Bruce Alexander and his colleagues questioned whether lab rats used morphine to self-medicate in response to the stress of being in such an unnatural and unpleasant environment.

To set up a fair test of this idea they set out to build the least-confining, most luxurious housing for rats that they could conceive of. They devised a large open-topped wooden box with plenty of floor space, including living areas and a climbing pole. A layer of sawdust provided opportunities for digging as well as absorbing ammonia from droppings. A group of young rats was introduced and was free to explore this socially and spatially rich environment, which became known as 'Rat Park'. Not so lucky was a second group of rats kept in standard lab conditions – they lived alone in small cages whose metal walls prevented visual contact with neighbouring creatures. Still, this second group was necessary in order to have a point of comparison in the research that followed. Both groups had access to clean water and a morphine drink. Over the following weeks, access to the morphine was controlled according to several different procedures designed to mimic different stages of drug addiction in humans.

Initially both water and morphine were available. Given the choice most preferred water regardless of whether they were housed in the park or the isolation cages. But then, for six weeks, all of the rats were provided only with morphine-laced drinking water, which meant that, essentially, the rats became drug users. However, on several days a choice between water and morphine was allowed. On these days, the isolated rats went on taking morphine while the social rats cut back significantly, by more than half. The experiment continued to run for several more weeks and during this time water and morphine drinks were provided on alternate days. This was a technique previously shown to increase the amount of morphine that lab rats would consume. Still, on choice days, when they could choose clean water, the isolated rats went on taking morphine but the socially housed rats cut back, this time by two-thirds. The experiment finished with the rats going 'cold turkey', in which only clean water was provided to drink. However, again, on days when choice was provided, the isolated rats had double the amount of morphine consumed by the social rats.

These findings show how general living conditions can play an important role in drug-taking. Even though all the rats in the study became 'users', on the days when they could choose between morphine solution or clean water, the isolated rats were much more likely to continue taking morphine than the rats living in the more pleasant, sociable surroundings of rat park. It seems that the social rats avoided morphine where possible because it interfered with their natural activity patterns. However, because these natural activities were already substantially curtailed by isolation, the rats in the small cages continued to take the morphine when they could. The usual explanation for addiction to morphine or heroin is that users persist in taking the drug to avoid unpleasant withdrawal effects. Yet, if this were true, then the socially housed rats should have continued to take morphine to the same level as the isolated rats. That they didn't indicates that an updated understanding of the nature of drug addiction, taking these findings into proper consideration, was required. But it's been a long time coming.

At the time the research was completed in the 1970s, Alexander struggled to find a research journal that would publish the results and within a few years of the article coming out his university withdrew its funding for his lab. Now Professor

Emeritus at Simon Fraser University in Canada, Bruce Alexander still vehemently disagrees with the official (biological) view of drug addiction. For one thing, if addiction were down to the biological properties of the substance being taken (heroin, alcohol or whatever) then how can we explain addictions to things like gambling, shopping and the Internet? Alexander argues that addiction is not something fundamentally drug-related, but instead any experience that sets off the brain's dopamine-rich reward pathways, like sex (see Chapter 1), eating chocolate or running can become addictive. He says that addictive drugs do not take over the normal willpower of individuals but it is convenient for people to believe this because it offers a convincing excuse for getting out of the trouble that often accompanies drug-taking. Finally, he says that addiction is not an incurable disease and that, actually, three-quarters of people who are described as drug addicts in their younger lives go on to a life without drugs, unaided by medical professionals.

How do they do this? They find that as they mature and establish stronger relations with the community or find a stronger sense of meaning in life, drugs become irrelevant. The quarter of people that find drugs harder to leave behind do so, in his view, because of their lifestyle and personal circumstances rather than any particular biological addictive power of the substances they use.

Still, there are signs that Alexander's views are beginning to make an impression on mainstream science. His recent book, *The Globalization of Addiction: A Study in Poverty of the Spirit*, received a 'high commendation' at the 2009 British Medical Association book awards. In addition, as I mentioned at the start of this section, for alcohol the American Psychiatric Association *Diagnostic and Statistical Manual of Mental Disorders* has gradually moved away from an addiction focus towards problem drinking, dropping the 'alcoholic' label in favour of a diagnosis that describes more specific difficulties in everyday life connected with alcohol. The same publication has also, for the first time, included 'gambling disorder' as an addictive disorder, recognizing Alexander's argument that addiction is not special to drugs, but that any highly enjoyable experience can become habit forming to the extent that it can disrupt a person's normal life and relationships.

So drink up – alcohol is one of a multitude of pleasurable activities, along with sex, chocolate and shopping, that are intrinsically enjoyable. Problem drinking does exist, of course, but the prevailing professional opinion is that it is a psychological problem rather than a chemical addiction. We have to exercise self-control to moderate our own excesses in alcohol, as in many other aspects of life. But if we can drink moderately, there are numerous scientifically verified benefits of alcohol consumption. Let's drink a toast to that.

Your good health

It's become well known that drinking a moderate amount of alcohol may be beneficial to health because it reduces the risk of heart disease and heart attacks. These claims arise from the findings of surveys completed by thousands of people showing that on the continuum from being teetotal through moderate drinking and into heavy drinking, health problems tend to be found at the ends of this continuum. Simply put, it is teetotallers and heavy drinkers who have the most risk of disease compared with moderate drinkers.

The Whitehall II study carried out by epidemiologists at University College London is a good example of this kind of study [see Britton & Marmot below]. The researchers asked a large group of people, in this case more than 10,000 London-based civil servants, a number of questions about their drinking habits. Then they waited for a long time – 14 years to be precise. Over that time some of the civil servants became ill, and a fair few died. The researchers accessed medical and work records to find out what caused the deaths and the nature of the illnesses suffered. The aim was to see if illness or death due to heart disease had any connection with the amount of alcohol typically consumed.

They found that people who died from heart disease were more likely to be very low or high consumers of alcohol, with fewer deaths among moderate alcohol consumers. In the UK, 1 unit of alcohol is a standard drink size containing 8g (10ml) of neat ethanol. Non-drinkers and those drinking more than 31 units per week (i.e. more than around 10 pints of strong 5% ABV beer or its equivalent) had twice the risk of dying from heart disease compared with moderate drinkers (drinking under 31 units per week). They also looked at how often people drank and noted that those drinking between once a week and once a day had a lower risk of heart disease. Drinking less often or more often than this, again, doubled the risk of heart disease. A similar survey in Spain [see Gea, below] found that compared with teetotallers, moderate drinkers (having 1-2 drinks per day) had a reduced risk of depression by around 40 per cent.

If you are a moderate drinker, studies like this are good news – the message that drinking alcohol, already considered pleasurable, also benefits health is very welcome. However, there is a raging and ongoing debate among researchers as to how reliable these findings are. The worry is that surveys of this kind do not provide a fair test of the link between alcohol and heart disease because of the complexity of carrying out 'real world' research such as this. The specific problem that is hard, if not impossible, to overcome is that there are many things that could be having an effect when one is looking at real people living their complex lives. The findings of these studies are, essentially, correlational; in other words, they have found two things in the world that happen together – being teetotal and having slightly higher levels of illness.

However, it does not always follow, when two things happen at the same time, that one caused the other and there are many examples of coincidental occurrences that are not causal. Take intelligence in children, for instance. Up to the age of about 18 years, intelligence increases year on year as the brain develops. Height also increases year on year as the body develops. If you only measured height and intelligence you would observe a correlation between the two that might tempt you to form a conclusion that being taller causes children to be more intelligent. This would be incorrect because a third variable – age – accounts for both height and intelligence.

The main criticism levelled at alcohol surveys showing health benefits for moderate drinkers over teetotallers is that moderate drinkers are generally a privileged and well-off group of people. In Western societies where these surveys are usually carried out, moderate drinking is a very normal part of everyday life. People who don't drink are unusual and have, to some extent, opted out of drinking. We don't know why but it could conceivably be because of underlying health issues. If so, then these underlying health issues may be the true cause of the increased risk in teetotallers rather than because of any protective effect of moderate drinking.

While studies like the Whitehall II study and the Spanish study take account of possibly important factors like age, smoking, obesity, and so on, there is a concern that they still do not sufficiently address the problems of inequality that are present in people filling in surveys as well as in wider society. The point is often made that only a **randomized controlled trial** can properly deal with these research design problems. A randomized controlled trial is a research technique in which, rather than have people choose themselves what or whether to drink (as the real life people who fill in a survey have done), instead people are randomly assigned to either alcohol or abstainer groups as part of a research project. They then spend a period of time drinking, or abstaining. When they are followed up, we can be more sure that alcohol underlies any effects (such as heart attacks) because the basis for choosing to drink (or not drink) alcohol was random, rather than due to reasons likely to influence the outcome, such as underlying health problems.

However, getting people to agree to take part in such a study would be impossible. Most moderate drinkers would be unwilling to give up alcohol for several years while the study was running and teetotallers would not welcome being asked to drink alcohol. That's why, to date, no such randomized controlled trial assessing the health benefits of alcohol has been carried out.

In the absence of this 'gold-standard' type of scientific evidence one is left wondering how accurate results of studies like the Whitehall II study really are. A recent report by the World Health Organization [*see* WHO, below] downplays the protective effects of alcohol, arguing that the level of benefit is lower and occurs at reduced levels of alcohol consumption than was previously thought. However, while it downplays them it does not go so far as to say they don't exist – rather it acknowledges that medical evidence supports health benefits of moderate alcohol consumption.

So a hidden benefit of alcohol is that, as far as researchers can tell, moderate drinking protects against problems like heart disease and depression. As long as it remains impossible to carry out long-term experiments with random assignment of volunteers this scientific view will most likely prevail. As we have seen, surveys are carried out in the real world and they tend, consequently, to be dirty, messy and uncontrollable in just the same way and for the same reasons that the world itself tends to be dirty, messy and uncontrollable. That's why it is generally much better, where possible, to conduct scientific experiments in the refined atmosphere of the laboratory. There the real world can be shut out, messiness can be kept to a minimum and control can be much more easily attained. Some fascinating, well-controlled laboratory experiments have discovered some much more tangible, less contested benefits of alcohol, as we shall see shortly.

The ideas game

Alcohol has been linked to the accomplishments of many great artistic individuals including Ludwig van Beethoven, F. Scott Fitzgerald and Jackson Pollock. The author J. G. Ballard was well known to use alcohol in the creative process of writing. Once asked where he got his ideas from, he enigmatically replied: 'Actually, there's no secret. One simply pulls the cork out of the bottle, waits three minutes, and two thousand or more years of Scottish craftsmanship does the rest.' [*see* Frick, below]. From F. Scott Fitzgerald to J. G. Ballard and from Jim Morrison to Amy Winehouse, alcohol and artists have always had a close association. But is there any scientific basis to the idea that alcohol can stimulate creativity?

Psychologists from the University of Illinois in Chicago thought so [*see* Jarosz et al, below]. First they needed to come up with a way of measuring creativity. They used a type of mental problem in which three words are presented (e.g. PEACH, ARM and TAR) and your task, if you want to solve the problem, is to think of the fourth word that connects all of the words together. Is this a suitable way to measure creativity? I think so because it mimics what often happens when we attempt to be creative in real life. If I was going to be creative, say, by writing a short story, it's likely that the first idea I had ('It was a dark and stormy night...') would not be very original and so I would have to put that idea aside and try to think of something else. It's similar with this three words task – the most obvious answers are often incorrect (e.g. TREE) and so to be successful you must be capable of forgetting that first response and generating other responses. Psychologically speaking, creativity problems often require a divergent style of thinking, leaping from one train of thought to another, as opposed to a more directed, logical thinking style in which you follow single trains of thought. To solve the three word task you need to leap from one idea to another to eventually find the word that the others have in common. You can check how agile your thought processes have been these past minutes – the solution to the PEACH, ARM, TAR problem is PIT.

The researchers gave a group of male social drinkers some alcohol – it was a vodka and cranberry juice drink. They wanted each volunteer to have about the same level of alcohol in their bloodstream and so the actual amount of vodka each person was given was measured in relation to their weight. This is because the bigger you are the greater your blood circulatory system and so the more alcohol that is needed to achieve the same concentration of blood alcohol. For a man of average weight the drink contained eight shots of vodka. The drinking time was deliberately short – half an hour – which would have sent blood alcohol levels rocketing. Here's a trivial but interesting detail: the paper mentions that while having their eight shots of vodka, the volunteers watched a DVD of one of my favourite Disney movies – *Ratatouille*. Blood alcohol levels peaked after one hour, at which point the DVD was stopped and the creativity testing got underway.

The vodka drinkers solved an average of 58 per cent of problems, which was an improvement over the 42 per cent solved by some other volunteers who were not given alcohol. And yet being tipsy had an impairing effect on the ability to control attention – the alcohol made the same volunteers much worse at remembering lists of words while at the same time doing maths problems. This is an important detail because the impairing effect of alcohol on the ability to control and direct one's attention seems to be what underlies the improvement in creativity. If this seems paradoxical, I'd agree. Usually, in most aspects of life, the ability to control attention is very useful, and disrupting it, by drinking or taking drugs, causes problems. However, thinking creatively can sometimes suffer if attention is directed *too much* because, as I said earlier, directing attention down a certain avenue (logically following a train of thought) may prevent exploring other avenues (divergently leaping from one train of thought to another) where a solution may reside.

So moderate alcohol consumption can boost your ability to think creatively, by changing how you control (or lose control of) your attention. Novelists like J. G. Ballard, who swore by the creative benefits of alcohol, have had their methods backed up by science. You could try this yourself. A thimbleful of whisky might give you an edge over the kids/parents next time you play Pictionary® or charades. Or you could try rereading a draft report for work or college after a glass of wine one evening, Maybe some new ideas will come to you; some different trains of thought that might help you link into novel areas that hadn't occurred before. Or maybe you should really let rip artistically and write a novel following the J. G. Ballard method – pouring yourself a glass of finest Scotch whisky and letting the ideas flow.

But, actually, would you want to drink alone like that? As said in the second half of Judge Sweat's famous speech, alcohol is recognized for its ability to draw people together and lubricate the cogs of social interaction. This could be more important than you think. There's a theory that alcohol is one of the foundations of civilization. Archaeologist Patrick McGovern has scoured the world searching for evidence of the history of human alcohol consumption [*see* McGovern, below]. He has a radical theory – that our first steps in agriculture cultivating cereals were motivated by beer production rather than bread. But then one thing followed another and with the technological advancements of organized agriculture and industrialization we gradually shifted from living in small social and family groups spread far and wide across the land with access to abundant, locally grown food, into city dwellers. Now we have become used to cohabiting cheek by jowl in sprawling cities in communities of millions. But here's a thought – isn't it unnatural for us to live in such close proximity to so many other people? What if city life is only bearable, indeed, only possible, thanks to the positive effects of the alcohol that has accompanied us on our journey into modernity. So is there any scientific evidence for alcohol being a prosocial drug?

Catching smiles

Have you ever noticed those people who, when you laugh, they laugh, or when you get angry, they get angry? Actually we all do this to some extent. The tendency for one person to mimic the emotion showed by another, often without realizing it, is known to psychologists as **emotional contagion**. This label is meant to convey the idea that emotions, like a virus, can be passed from one person to another, creating a feeling of unity and togetherness – a kind of 'social glue'. While very common in social situations, some people deliberately stop themselves from copying the emotions of the other members in a group. These people are called men.

The reason why men actively suppress the natural urge to reflect the emotions of other people is connected to ideas around masculinity, and what it means to be a man, that are part of Western culture. When men get together the conversation tends to revolve around competence and status with very few instances of men showing intimacy or affection for one another. This is in stark contrast to women, who not only have more friends and larger social networks than men, but also show more support and responsiveness to the needs of others during social interactions. Psychologists from the University of Pittsburgh wondered whether alcohol, by interfering with the control of attention, might help men to become better social mimickers [*see* Fairbairn et al, below].

On the whole this must rank as one of the more pleasant studies to take part in. Volunteers were paid, they had several vodkas and cranberry juice (or just cranberry juice with a few drops of vodka floated on the surface if they were in the no-alcohol group) and they got to sit about, drinking and chatting. On the other hand, I'm glad not to have been part of the researcher team. They had the very laborious task of going through video film of these social interactions frame by frame – and there were a whopping 34.9 million frames in total. The researchers were taking note of who was smiling and they were particularly on the lookout for smiles spreading around the group from person to person. This is where one person smiles at another, and the first person smiles back. Interestingly, compared with all-male groups, adding a woman increased the number of times that smiles spread around the group by 9 per cent. However, feminine charms were overshadowed by vodka. Introducing alcohol to all-male groups increased the number of times that smiles spread around the group by a far larger 21 per cent.

But what does it mean to catch a smile? Men and women who caught smiles more often, even without realizing it, felt a greater sense of social bonding. This shows that smile catching is a rewarding activity with tangible benefits. Men don't naturally take to smile catching or other displays of emotional contagion but drinking alcohol enabled them to loosen up and join in. Alcohol is renowned as a social drug and here is some science demonstrating a social enhancement effect. I wouldn't go as far as saying that it puts men in touch with their feminine side but this research shows that moderate drinking helps men to relax and better enjoy male company. And it doesn't stop there. Alcohol also bolsters social relations between the sexes but in a completely different way. Ever heard of beer goggles?

Being original and funny

It's long been known that drinking alcohol makes members of the opposite sex seem more physically attractive. Psychologists from Glasgow University are credited with the first scientific recording of this so-called 'beer goggles' effect [see Jones et al, below]. Actually, describing this research as 'scientific' seems a little over the top given what actually happened was some researchers trawled a university's bars for inebriated students and asked them to rate, on a 1-7 scale, the attractiveness of some photographs of faces. Still, they were systematic and they found, in heterosexual moderate drinkers (they'd had no more than six units), an opposite sex enhancement of attractiveness ratings due to alcohol. In other words, women who had been drinking rated the male faces as more attractive overall than women who had not been drinking, and vice versa for males rating female faces. Finding people attractive is a first step to approaching them so this is another example of alcohol as social glue. The research indicates that one reason why alcohol makes you more sociable is that it just makes people look nicer.

But does this only apply to how we perceive others or could this be a more fundamental effect? Some psychologists from Grenoble, Ohio, Amsterdam and Paris turned the tables on the beer goggles research [see Bègue et al, below]. They asked not whether alcohol altered how attractive we find others, but whether it made people seem more attractive to themselves. Here the question was – does alcohol make you a narcissist?

They asked customers at a bar in Grenoble, France, to rate how attractive, bright, original and funny they felt they were, and then asked them to blow into a breathalyser to measure their blood alcohol levels. As you might have guessed, the higher the blood alcohol level the more attractive, bright, original and funny people thought themselves to be.

There's a saying: the answer may not lie in the bottom of a bottle, but sometimes it can't hurt to check. These research studies tell us that by disrupting the ability to control attention alcohol can be socially beneficial. Moderate alcohol consumption can make you seem more attractive to yourself, make others seem more attractive to you and help men to relate better to one another. These prosocial effects would certainly ease the claustrophobia of modern city life. Alcohol consumption has accompanied the industrialization that has brought so many people together in cities. Could our cities function without alcohol? How would crime statistics look without the ale that puts songs in hearts and laughter on lips?

And yet, and yet... alcohol sits on a knife edge. There will always be positive and negative sides to its consumption. We can so quickly flip from the philosophic wine to the poison scourge. And that's certainly true of the loss of attentional control that underlies the prosocial effects of alcohol just mentioned. When attention is impaired so is our usual tendency to monitor and alter what we do and say, making us less likely to take into account social etiquette and the opinions and feelings of other people. Freed from these social constraints by alcohol, people do things and say things that they normally would not. This kind of social disinhibition has mixed consequences. It can help people feel more confident, but too much alcohol can lead to an annoying, misjudged overconfidence. Where alcohol is concerned, the tricky thing is how to moderate; how to stop drinking once you've started. Thankfully, there is a 'stop' button built in to the whole alcohol ritual. It is illustrated very clearly by the author Kingsley Amis in his 1954 novel *Lucky Jim*:

'*A dusty thudding in his head made the scene before him beat like a pulse. His mouth had been used as a latrine by some small creature of the night and then as its mausoleum… He resolved, having done it once, never to move his eyeballs again.*'

The morning after the night before

Earlier I mentioned a study in which volunteers got to watch a DVD of the Disney Pixar film *Ratatouille* while they drank vodka and cranberry juice – all in the name of research! I explained how they watched for one hour while their blood alcohol levels climbed steadily. Assuming they started at the beginning, the film would have stopped just at the point where trainee chef Linguini is seen crashing around the kitchen with a dreadful hangover, having been plied with wine the previous evening. Kingsley Amis's description would suffice well to describe Linguini's suffering – although in this instance the lines about what a small creature of the night may or may not have done are given a whole new set of possibilities when we remember big chef Linguini's on-screen partnership with little chef Remy the rat!

A scientific understanding of alcohol hangovers is in its infancy compared with alcohol research more generally. Science has discovered much about being drunk (or more properly, alcohol intoxication effects that occur while alcohol is still being carried around the body in the bloodstream) and the longer-term effects associated with years of heavy drinking. Hangovers, on the other hand, have been a neglected topic of serious scientific study, which is odd given their prominence in the experience of drinking alcohol. A very important question around hangovers is whether they serve any useful purpose.

A popular view of hangovers is that they provide a natural buffer to prevent excessive alcohol consumption. This view of hangovers as an 'opponent process' assumes that hangovers encourage our bodies to take action against a harmful exposure – in this case intoxication due to alcohol.

On the other hand, a hangover might actually encourage further drinking in order to relieve its unpleasant symptoms. There is a scientific basis for the so-called 'hair of the dog' hangover cure. In the late 1990s a team from Sweden [see Bendtsen et al, below) got some hospital employees first to drink their choice of white wine or beer and then to pee into a bottle several times over the next few hours. Methanol levels in urine peaked in the first morning sample, coinciding with when the hangover symptoms of headache and nausea were at their most severe. This shows how methanol, present in alcoholic beverages in small amounts, is one biological cause of alcohol hangover. The body breaks down methanol into toxic substances that make us feel ill. Interestingly, both ethanol, the alcohol that we enjoy in our beers, wines and spirits, and methanol are broken down in the body by the same enzyme, alcohol dehydrogenase. However, the enzyme 'prefers' ethanol over methanol and so, during a hangover, flooding one's system with ethanol by drinking more alcohol will slow down the toxic metabolism of methanol. This is the biological basis for the 'hair of the dog'.

Discovering whether a hangover is our friend because it helps us to curb excessive alcohol consumption, or our enemy because it makes us want to drink more, is an important research question. However, the need, rightly, to protect the health of research volunteers means that the amount of alcohol allowed in laboratory studies is strictly limited to no more than around 6 bottles of beer or the equivalent of this. This creates the problem that the more 'full blown' hangover effects arising from extensive alcohol consumption can't properly be studied under laboratory conditions. Researchers from the University of Aarhus in Copenhagen took a rather different and novel approach [*see* Hesse & Tutenges, below].

Sunny Beach on the Black Sea is the largest beach resort in Bulgaria. Marketed as 'The sunniest resort for the sunniest people', it attracts many thousands of tourists each year who flock there to relax and enjoy the sandy beach and nightlife. Particularly the nightlife. With its numerous pubs, bars, clubs, cafes and discos, Sunny Beach visitors regularly drink to excess in pursuit of party fun. There is, of course, a downside to this kind of behaviour. By the next morning the highs of the liquor-fuelled bender give way to the lows of the alcohol hangover. A raging thirst, headache, feelings of nausea and being unable to stomach food are its hallmarks; the symptoms of alcohol hangover are unmistakable.

In the name of science four lucky University of Aarhus research assistants were dispatched to the resort one summer. They were free to enjoy the location, and basically had a free summer-long holiday, provided they carried out some research duties each day. They had to rise bright and early and visit the many hotels, swimming pools and beaches up and down the bay with the aim of chatting to as many young Danish holidaymakers as they could find. They had several questions for the vacationers. They wanted descriptions of their nights out, a list of all the drinks they'd had, and last but not least, they wanted to know whether they were suffering from a hangover. Crucially, each person was spoken to three times, at the start, middle and end of their week-long holiday. This allowed the researchers to chart how hangovers progress over time in the face of continued drinking.

The researchers were particularly interested in the relationship between the amount people drank and the extent of the resulting hangover. They reasoned that if hangovers act as a natural curb on drinking, that is if a hangover is an 'opponent process' to further drinking, then they would expect to see either decreased alcohol consumption or increased symptoms of hangover over the week, or some combination of the two. So, in this environment of sun, sea, sand and alcohol-fuelled partying, where numerous holidaymakers consume astonishing amounts of alcohol, what did we learn about the science of hangovers?

For these Danish holidaymakers the amount of alcohol consumed per night was more or less the same at the start, middle and end of their week-long holiday. They drank an average of 17 standard units of alcohol on average each night. This is like drinking ten standard-sized bottles of beer, and would be enough to give most people a hangover the next morning. I should also add that this quantity of alcohol exceeds moderate drinking and if sustained would lead to health problems. While the amount of alcohol consumed was about the same for most people, hangover severity increased over the week, with the average hangover rating rising each time they were interviewed. This is the opposite of what we would have expected to see if there were such a thing as hangover tolerance, which is the idea that we can 'get used' to hangovers so that we gradually feel them less strongly. Hangovers getting worse over the duration of the holiday, in the face of similar levels of alcohol consumption, favour the 'opponent process' idea of hangover being part of the body's response of preserving itself from harm by reducing the appetite for further intake of toxins like alcohol.

Although saying that it favours the opponent process idea is not to say that it directly supports it. For hangover to be an effective 'opponent process' to excessive drinking we would want to see evidence that it exerts some influence on future drinking. This was not the case at Sunny Beach where nightly alcohol consumption stayed the same. However, a recent electronic diary study at Missouri University [see Epler et al, below] used a software app on a pocket-sized electronic device that prompted volunteers to record what they were drinking while they were on nights out. The app also functioned like an alarm clock, awakening them the next morning and getting them to record any signs of hangover. Because they carried the app with them for three weeks the researchers were able to look at a new variable that had not before been assessed in hangover research – the time until the next drink. This provides an excellent means of directly assessing whether having a hangover has an influence on subsequent drinking. If hangover is an opponent process to alcohol then the more severe a hangover that is experienced the greater should be the time until the next drink.

Among these diary keepers it was found that having a hangover did delay the time to the next drink by a small amount – around six hours. However, the researchers were not very confident in this finding because it was overtaken by the much stronger influence of drinking habits. In other words, how often people drank and the day of the week that the diary entry was made were much more strongly related to when volunteers would next drink compared with hangover. The relationships were such that heavier drinking often predicted a shorter time to the next drink, and filling in the survey on Friday predicted a shorter time to the next drink, while on a Sunday it predicted a longer time to the next drink.

Nevertheless, it certainly wasn't the case that having a hangover led to a *shorter* time to the next drink, so the idea that a hangover encourages hair of the dog drinking on any significant scale can be set aside. Research has still not been carried out to look at whether the perceived threat of a hangover influences how much people drink. In other words, we don't have a clear idea of whether people moderate what they drink with tomorrow's potential hangover in mind. The closest to this was a survey of the medical school students and staff at State University of New York in Buffalo [*see* Smith et al, below], over half of whom reported that they had drunk less in order to avoid a hangover; but this could be a case of people saying one thing but actually doing another – a study assessing actual drinking behaviour is called for.

Overall, there is some scientific evidence to support the idea that hangover can be a natural brake to drinking excessive amounts of alcohol but more research is needed. I started off this section saying that there had been very little research on hangovers compared with other aspects of drinking alcohol and this point illustrates this.

The Sunny Beach study reveals some further intriguing findings. It's generally assumed that women get worse hangovers than men but at first glance the opposite seemed to be the case in Sunny Beach. However, there was an obvious reason why the women's hangovers were less severe than the men's – because the women tended to drink less than the men. There turned out to be no difference between men's and women's level of hangover symptoms when the amount of alcohol consumed was taken into account. The general belief that women get worse hangovers than men is probably down to the fact that women, generally, have lower body mass than men. If women and men drank the same amount you'd expect women to have a more severe hangover because women would have had a larger 'dose' of alcohol than the men, taking body mass into account.

Another widely held belief is that older people get worse hangovers than younger people – but this also seems not to be so. At Sunny Beach, hangover symptoms were less severe in the older people that were questioned, although don't forget that the entire sample were young adults and so 'older' in this context means late 20s. But a large-scale Danish survey of more than 50,000 adults across the full age range (teens to over-60s), which I helped to write up, also showed that hangovers are more a young person's problem [see Tolstrup et al, below]. The survey found that the older people became, the fewer hangovers they experienced. This can be explained as an 'older and wiser' effect; as we get older we learn strategies to avoid hangovers including moderating how much we drink. So it seems that the 'stop signal' message from hangover to drink sensibly may be heeded more the older we get.

But hangovers are not the same for everybody. A further fascinating finding from Sunny Beach centred on hangover immunity – that is, whether there are some people who never get hangovers regardless of how much they drink. Focusing only on those holidaymakers who drank enough to get a hangover the next day, the research found that only around two-thirds of these heavy drinkers actually experienced a hangover. This means that around one-third of people may be immune from hangovers. Actually this estimate is a little higher than other studies have found. Psychologists from Boston University examined many different hangover studies and concluded that around 23 per cent of the population don't get hangovers, whatever they drink [see Howland et al, below]. Of course, hangover immunity is not as lucky as you might at first think because if you never get a hangover then you can't benefit from its moderating effect on drinking.

One of my aims in writing this book is to showcase the many innovative and interesting things that psychology researchers get up to in their professional lives. The Sunny Beach hangover study is a great example. It was a simple, yet inspired idea to fly researchers to a beach holiday resort in order to collect data related to excessive alcohol consumption. I just wish I'd thought of this straightforward approach. The findings too are very easy to understand and apply to everyday life. Hangovers don't ease over time, they get worse. But this worsening of hangovers with continued drinking provides a message that we can heed to reduce our future alcohol consumption. Some people don't heed the message. The very young don't, but they will in time. The 23 per cent of drinkers who don't get hangovers at all don't have the opportunity to learn from hangovers. Are they lucky? In some ways yes, since they can drink to excess and get off lightly the next day. However, without the 'opponent process' or natural curb to excessive drinking that hangover provides, perhaps such individuals are more at risk from developing harmful patterns of alcohol consumption storing up possible health problems as they get older. Now there's a sobering thought.

Last orders

Alcohol is both angel and demon; hero and villain. It's very difficult to provide a definitive statement about whether alcohol is good or bad because it is so interwoven into our lives that disentangling its positive and negative effects is very difficult. Science and medicine want to get it right, or at least do no harm, and so tend to err on the side of caution, declaring drinking to be universally bad and best avoided. And yet, alcohol consumption remains popular. Why? I think it's because people already know the (not so) hidden benefits – they don't need someone like me to spell them out. Science hasn't always got it right in relation to the complex phenomenon of alcohol. That's illustrated by the gradual rethink of how alcohol problems are diagnosed, moving away from terms like 'dependence' to the currently favoured 'alcohol use disorder' which recognizes problem drinking as more of a psychological than a biological issue.

There's little doubt that excessive alcohol consumption, including binge drinking with the aim of getting drunk, will compromise health. But the message of this chapter is that there are numerous not-so-hidden benefits of moderate drinking. Some of these are health related, protecting against heart disease and depression. Others, paradoxically, are related to alcohol's disruptive influence on attention. Alcohol can make you creative and more prosocial, and what's more it has its own 'off' button, otherwise known as the dreaded hangover. Enjoy a drink – but not to the point that you find yourself waking up with small creatures, animated or otherwise, entombed in your mouth.

Further reading

Alexander, B. K., Coambs, R. B & Hadaway, P. F. (1978), 'The effect of housing and gender on morphine self-administration in rats. *Psychopharmacology*, Vol. 58 pp 175–9

Bègue, L., Bushman, B. J., Zerhouni, O., Subra, B. & Ourabah, M. (2013), 'Beauty is in the eye of the beer holder: People who think they are drunk also think they are attractive', *British Journal of Psychology*, Vol. 104 Issue 2 pp 225–34

Bendtsen, P., Jones, A.W. & Helander, A. (1998), 'Urinary excretion of methanol and 5-hydroxytryptophol as biochemical markers of recent drinking in the hangover state', *Alcohol & Alcoholism*, Vol. 33 Issue 4 pp 431–8

Britton, A. & Marmot, M. (2004), 'Different measures of alcohol consumption and risk of coronary heart disease and all-cause mortality: 11-year follow-up of the Whitehall II Cohort Study', *Addiction*, Vol. 99 Issue 1 pp 109–116

Epler, A. J., Tomko, R.L., Piasecki, T.M., Wood, P.K., Sher, K.J., Shiffman, S. & Heath, A. C. (2014), 'Does Hangover Influence the Time to Next Drink? An investigation using ecological momentary assessment', *Alcoholism: Clinical and Experimental Research*, Vol. 38 Issue 5 pp 1461–9

Fairbairn, C. E., Sayette, M. A., Aalen, O. O. & Frigessi, A. (2014), 'Alcohol and Emotional Contagion: An Examination of the Spreading of Smiles in Male and Female Drinking Groups', *Clinical Psychological Science*

Frick, T. (1984), 'Interviews: J. G. Ballard, The Art of Fiction No. 85'. From: www.theparisreview.org/interviews/2929/the-art-of-fiction-no-85-j-g-ballard

Gea et al (2013), 'Alcohol intake, wine consumption and the development of depression: the PREDIMED study', *BMC Medicine* 2013, Vol. 11 pp 192

Grohol, J. M. (2015), 'DSM-5 changes: Addiction, substance-related disorders & alcoholism'. From: http://pro.psychcentral.com/dsm-5-changes-addiction-substance-related-disorders-alcoholism/004370.html#

Hesse, M. & Tutenges, S. (2010), 'Predictors of hangover during a week of heavy drinking on holiday', *Addiction*, Vol. 105 Issue 3 pp 476-83

Howland, J., Rohsenow D. J. & Edwards, E. M. (2008), 'Are Some Drinkers Resistant to Hangover? A Literature Review', *Current Drug Abuse Reviews*, Vol. 1 Issue 1 pp 42–6

Jarosz, A. F., Colflesh, G. J. & Wiley, J. (2012), 'Uncorking the muse: alcohol intoxication facilitates creative problem solving', *Consciousness and cognition*, Vol. 21 Issue 1 pp 487–93

Jones, B. T., Jones, B.C., Thomas, A. P. & Piper, J. (2003), 'Alcohol consumption increases attractiveness ratings of opposite-sex faces: a possible third route to risky sex', *Addiction*, Vol. 98 Issue 8 pp 1069–75

McGovern, Patrick E., *Uncorking the past: The quest for wine, beer and other alcoholic beverages* (University of California Press, Berkeley, 2009)

National Institute on Alcohol Abuse and Alcoholism (1995), 'Diagnostic Criteria for Alcohol Abuse and Dependence', *Alcohol Alert* No. 30 PH 359. From: http://pubs.niaaa.nih.gov/publications/aa30.htm

NIH (2013), 'Alcohol Use Disorder: A Comparison Between DSM–IV and DSM–5', *NIH Publication* No. 13–7999. From: pubs.niaaa.nih.gov/publications/dsmfactsheet/dsmfact.htm

Pain, S. (2008), 'When doctors battled for medical beer', *New Scientist*, Issue 2680. From: www.newscientist.com/article/mg20026801.900-when-doctors-battled-for-medical-beer.html

Smith, C., Bookner, S. & Dreher, F. (1988), 'Effects of alcohol intoxication and hangovers on subsequent drinking', *Problems of Drug Dependence 1988: Proceedings of the 50th Annual Scientific Meeting*' (NIDA, Harris, L. S., ed.), p 366

Tolstrup, J., Stephens, R. & Grønbæk, M. (2014), 'Does the severity of hangovers decline with age? Survey of the incidence of severe hangover in different age groups', *Alcoholism: Clinical and Experimental Research*, Vol. 38 Issue 2 pp 466–70

WHO (2012), 'European action plan to reduce the harmful use of alcohol 2012–2020', Copenhagen: WHO Regional Office for Europe

3

Damn good

It was the 2008 Olympic Games in Beijing and Britain's female windsurfers had never before won a medal. That year's event was fiercely contested by 27 sailors from 27 nations and there was high drama in the final race. It began with a false start and part of the way around the course one of the medallists was almost knocked into the sea by another competitor. This backdrop of adversity can only have added to the immense joy experienced by Britain's Bryony Shaw when, against all expectations, she finished third and took the bronze medal. Emerging from the water still dripping wet, the BBC thrust her before a microphone, a camera and a millions-strong live television audience. Asked how she was feeling at this incredible moment, the understandably ecstatic Shaw must have felt at a loss for words. Instinctively, she reached for a register of verbal expression that could truly do justice to conveying the dizzying whirl of emotion at that climactic moment. To the consternation of the BBC producer in charge that afternoon, she unabashedly exclaimed: 'I'm so *fucking* happy!' [*see The Daily Telegraph*, below].

The use of offensive, obscene or taboo language is a linguistic feature in most human cultures, from the English *fuck off* to the French *merde* (shit) and from the Indian *sala* (brother-in-law) to the Arabic *yil3an abu ommak* (curse your grandfather). While people tend to think of the 'four-letter words' as a modern phenomenon, the reality is that the earliest recorded uses of these words date from 1,000 years ago (*fuck* is one of the most recent, at c. 1503)[*see* Hughes, below]. Some of the stories around swear words are fascinating. For example, *cunt* first appeared in a written-down form c. 1230 in the London street name 'Gropecuntlane' – this appellation reflecting a location frequented by prostitutes and their clients as well as a public acceptability of the word at that time. The word was also used in medical writing in the 1400s. *Arse* first appeared in English at c. 1000. Its close resemblance to the word *ass*, the eeyorring beast of burden, was unfortunate. Imagine the amusement and embarrassment ensuing from previously innocent musings, like 'I was admiring your ass the other day'. That explains why, after arse made its appearance, so did the word donkey [*see* Hughes, below]

But while swearing can often be negative, ugly and con-frontational there is no doubt that there are forms of swearing that are palatable and perhaps even necessary. This chapter will explore the science of bad language and particularly the many hidden benefits of swearing. These include: to express emotion, as a tool for persuasion, as a means of coping with pain, as a way of identifying dementia and, believe it or not, to be polite. There's much more to swearing than meets the eye (or ear).

The when

In the late 1950s a group of university zoologists went on a field trip to Arctic Norway. They were there to observe how birds coped with continuous daylight. However, things didn't always go smoothly – scrambling over rocks and cliffs to capture and ring wild birds, erecting tents, cooking and other tasks became that much harder in the unforgiving arctic climate. This made it an ideal environment for a trainee psychologist to observe when (and subsequently deduce why) the five men and three women on the expedition swore. And so it was that for several hours per day, the number of swear words uttered by each member of the group was tracked by the trainee psychologist using some

FIGURE 3.1 Knitting needle counter

exceedingly low-tech science equipment – differently coloured knitting needle counters. The findings were written up in a report that became the first published systematic study of swearing produced by a psychologist [*see* Ross, below].

It turns out that these zoologists swore for two quite different reasons. On one hand, the amount of swearing increased markedly when people were relaxed and happy. Labelled as 'social swearing', this was intended to be friendly, was a sign of being 'one of the gang', and only occurred when there was an audience. On the other hand, when things went wrong a second type of swearing was evident. Labelled 'annoyance swearing', this occurred in relation to mild stress (e.g. losing one's way), was rarer than social swearing and it didn't require an audience. Interestingly, as the stress became more severe (e.g. losing one's way for a prolonged length of time) swearing of both types – annoyance and social – reduced. It's a lovely piece of research not least for its being so far ahead of the field, considering that swearing is only now taking off as a serious topic of scientific study. However, while I applaud the very low-tech approach, it was not without its problems. Midway through the field trip, the zoologists realized what was happening due to the giveaway clicking sound of the knitting counters. This led to the coining of a new swearword among the group, *clicking*, which was quickly appropriated into more complex linguistic expressions such as, 'oh that *clicking* psychologist!'.

Still, the two basic kinds of swearing that were identified ring true and, actually, these were confirmed more recently when some Australian linguists analysed a collection of examples of Antipodean written and spoken language [*see* Allan & Burridge, below]. They examined sources including the Internet (e.g. the Myspace social networking website), pieces of creative writing, spontaneous public speech and private conversation. This more up-to-date study identified four types of swearing. These were 'social swearing' where no offence is intended (e.g. '*I didn't know what the fuck I was wearing*'), 'annoyance swearing' (e.g. '*Oh shit I'm getting lost*'), 'abusive swearing' (e.g. '*the people on night fills are arseholes*') and 'stylistic swearing', which is the use of bad language to spice up what is being said (e.g. '*Welfare, my arsehole*').

So science has done a reasonable job of documenting when people swear – in social situations (and I would add the 'spicing up' function in that category), when annoyed and to be deliberately abusive. You could add swearing out of habit to the list – which is a kind of swearing that may have initially arisen for social reasons but has become so ingrained in a speaker's vocabulary that it happens now for no discernible reason at all. This kind of rapid-fire, meaningless and indiscriminate swearing has spawned the popular idea that swearing is a sign of low intelligence and inarticulateness. However, this is not as straightforward an idea as you might expect and, actually, some very good evidence provided by a further study of written and spoken English points to the contrary.

The who

Linguists from Lancaster University in the UK were interested in how the word *fuck* and its derivatives (e.g. *fucked, fucks, fucking, fucker*) was used by men and women of different ages and from different social groups [*see* McEnery & Xiao, below]. They carried out a study based on a resource known as the *British National Corpus*. This is a 100-million-word collection of samples of written and spoken English assembled from late-20th-century sources. The written samples came from sources such as newspapers, books and private letters. The spoken samples came from conversations recorded by volunteers. The researchers explain that they chose *fuck* because of its status as one of the most interesting and colourful words in the English language, which is nicely illustrated by the variety of usage types that were encountered in the samples. These included the 'general expletive' (oh *fuck!*), the 'personal insult' (you *fuck!*), the 'cursing expletive' (*fuck* you!), the 'literal usage' (he *fucked* her), the 'emphatic intensifier' (*fucking* marvellous!), the 'pronominal form' (like *fuck*), the 'idiomatic set phrase' (*fuck* all) and, last but not least, the hilariously labelled 'destinational usage' (*fuck* off!).

Men used *fuck* and its derivatives twice as often as women, confirming the popular belief that men swear more than women (although this is contested – a recent study found it was 50/50 [*see* Jay & Jay, below]). Looking across age groups, the under-35s used *fuck* much more frequently than the over-35s, possibly because the older group have children and teenagers around them and temper their language accordingly. A very crude measure of educational level of the speakers was their school leaving age. Swearing (use of the word *fuck*) decreased by 84 per cent from leaving school at 15-16 to leaving school at 17-18 and decreased a further 66 per cent from leaving school at 17-18 to staying in education beyond age 18. This shows a clear link between swearing frequency and educational level, with swearing being more common in those who leave school earlier. This partly supports the low IQ and inarticulateness explanation of why people swear, assuming that, in general, IQ is lower in people that leave school earlier. However, some further probing indicates that this may be too simple an explanation.

When the researchers looked at swearing in relation to social class the picture at first seemed similar, with the highest level of swearing in the lower classes. Swearing reduced by 24 per cent from the non-working and unskilled to the skilled working class, and then by a whopping 85 per cent from the skilled working class to the lower middle class (clerical workers and junior professional positions). However, moving further up the social ladder something very odd happened. From the lower middle class to the upper middle class (higher managerial and professional positions), the use of *fuck* actually increased by 300 per cent, indicating an upturn in swearing at the very top of the social ladder. The explanation for this may be an effect whereby the aspirational lower middle classes moderate their language in order to conform to the social ideal for which they are striving, whereas the more secure upper middle classes don't care and so they swear much more freely. You could say that they just don't *give a fuck*.

What this study shows, then, is that there is more to swearing than inarticulateness and low IQ. If swearing were only a matter of IQ and vocabulary skills, then we should not be seeing this rise in swearing in higher managerial and professional workers; whatever you may think of this social group, they couldn't be low in intelligence and verbal ability and retain these authoritative positions for long.

A final nail in the coffin of the idea that swearing is a product of inarticulateness comes from a recently published study by psychologists from Massachusetts College of Liberal Arts (MCLA) [*see* Jay & Jay, below]. In it they compared general language fluency with swearing fluency. General language fluency can be measured by asking volunteers to think of (and write down) as many words as they can in one minute beginning with certain letters of the alphabet. People with greater language skills can generally think of more example words in the allotted time. Cleverly, the researchers devised a test of 'swearing fluency' along similar lines. The Swearing Fluency Task requires the thinking up of as many different swear words as possible in one minute. When people's scores on the two tests were compared it was found that the people who did best on the general language fluency test were also fluent at swearing, and the weakest did poorly on both tests. This strongly indicates that swearing is not simply a sign of language poverty (i.e. the lack of general vocabulary) but instead is one of the many features of language that a skilled and articulate speaker has at their disposal to communicate with maximum effectiveness.

So science has given us an understanding of when people swear and what kinds of people swear. But we are still some way off understanding why they do it – and what the hidden benefits of swearing are. The answer seems to be that we have a specific and involuntary response to swearing. It's an emotional response using the same brain pathways that process fear and surprise.

Fight or flight

I've given numerous talks on the science of swearing over the years. You don't actually have to use swear words to speak about them and I have at times got through an entire talk without swearing, such as one time when I spoke at a science festival with very young children in the audience (who, incidentally, were just as fascinated by the science of swearing as the adults). However, I feel it adds a little to the novelty and interest of the topic to introduce a smattering of bad language. There's something quite satisfying in articulating a well-placed '*fuck*' in front of a hushed audience in a hallowed university lecture theatre. A colleague who attended one my presentations told me that the moment the first swear word was spoken she felt a small jolt of energy – a *frisson* you could say. That's a good illustration of the power of swearing. It's also an accurate description of what it feels like when your body's 'fight or flight' response is activated.

The fight or flight response is our most fundamental stress reaction and consists of a series of tweaks to our biology that enhance action. The most important tweak is to generate a burst of energy that can be used in an emergency, such as an attack, giving us the best possible chance of survival through fighting off the attacker or swiftly running away. Its hallmark is the release of adrenaline that sets the heart pumping. It causes dilation of the pupils, more rapid breathing and faster heart rate, as well as increased pain tolerance and sweating. This last property, sweating, is interesting from a science point of view. Because moisture conducts electricity, the more sweaty you are the more readily your skin can conduct an electric current. The level of conductivity at any one time can be measured using electrodes taped to the fingers, and is known as 'electrodermal response'.

A number of studies have measured the degree of *frisson* produced by swearing via this electrodermal response. Researchers from Bristol University in the UK had volunteers read aloud the words *cunt* and *fuck*, compared with *c-word* and *f-word* [*see* Bowers & Pleydell-Pearce, below]. Researchers from MCLA asked volunteers to read silently a number of swear words and animal words [*see* Jay, Caldwell-Harris & King, below].

Finally, psychologists from Yale University had volunteers read emotionally arousing words consisting of profanities, sexually explicit words and social taboos [*see* LaBar & Phelps, below]. They all showed greater electrodermal response to the swear words compared with the politer expressions. These studies, and the frisson experienced by my colleague, show that swearing is, or at least can be, emotional language. To explain the links between swearing and emotion we will consider what it is to break the social taboo of swearing – and so it is that we must now delve into the neurobiology of filthy words.

Pissing, shitting, fucking, cocks and cunts

We all carry around with us in our memories a repertoire of swear words and phrases such as those that I have rather gratuitously listed in the subheading. We know these words but we don't go around saying them all the time because it's embarrassing in polite company to remind everyone that, like it or not, we remain animals that urinate, defecate and have sexual relations. This is one reason why swearing is taboo. Breaking that taboo by mentioning this stuff just puts everyone on edge that little bit and makes us feel a little more vulnerable. On top of that, we grow up around elders that, to greater or lesser extents, swear. Since childhood we have learned to associate swearing with the emotionally charged situations in which it tends to be most prominent, such as injury, conflict and perhaps violence. So swearing also awakens ideas that a drama may be about to unfold and makes us feel uneasy for that reason. Swearing adds an edge to proceedings because of its links with our more primitive selves and by association with previous adrenaline-prompting situations. This is one reason why swearing can provoke an emotional response.

In addition, there's evidence that swearing is handled differently by the brain compared with regular language. Researchers from the University of Southern California produced a type of research known as a 'literature review', in which they pulled together findings from a range of research areas connected with swearing [*see*Van Lancker & Cummings, below]. They included research on patients with a language disorder known as **aphasia**, studies of monkeys and findings from patients with Gilles de la Tourette syndrome, otherwise known as **Tourette's**.

People with aphasia have difficulty speaking in a meaningful way. Some aphasics can hardly speak at all due to a condition known as **Broca's aphasia**. Others can speak very rapidly but the stream of words they produce does not make any sense, which happens due to **Wernicke's aphasia**. Examining the brains of aphasia patients has revealed that most have brain damage to the left **cerebral cortex** (the crinkly folded-over-on-itself surface of the brain where our most complex intellectual thinking takes place) just above the left ear. This distinctive pattern of brain damage supports the idea that language is associated with these damaged brain regions. However, fascinatingly, despite the general difficulties with language that aphasics have, some patients can still swear fluently. There are documented cases of otherwise impaired individuals being able to say curse phrases such as *Sacre nom de Dieu, Jesus Christ* and *Goddammit*. That individuals with brain damage to key language areas can nevertheless swear indicates that compared with regular language, swearing is a special case.

Some further evidence that swearing is different to normal language comes from studies of macaque and squirrel monkeys. Researchers have used a technique in which different parts of the brains of animals are directly stimulated with very low voltage electrical currents. The currents are low enough not to cause damage but sufficient to activate neurons (brain cells). The interest lies in seeing what the monkeys do when their neurons are directly stimulated in this manner.

Direct stimulation of deeper brain structures of these animals, that is, parts of the brain situated towards the centre, rather than the cerebral cortex at the outermost surface, produced emotional vocalizations. These were short, staccato shrieks normally used to warn other members of the troop that danger may be present. The particular region that produced these vocalizations after electrical stimulation was a known emotional centre in the brain called the **limbic system**. Some kinds of swearing in humans, particularly emotional outbursts when people are upset, resemble these emotional vocalizations of macaque and squirrel monkeys. Perhaps human swearing may also be dependent on the limbic system. In fact, evidence from Tourette's patients indicates that this may be the case.

The swearing tic that epitomizes Tourette's in the public eye is known as **coprolalia**. Actually, the majority of Tourette's patients don't have coprolalia, although a significant proportion do, estimated at between 25 per and 50 per cent. Numerous studies indicate that, compared with non-sufferers, Tourette's patients have smaller **basal ganglia**, which are another deeplying brain region. This led the researchers from the University of Southern California, who produced the literature review, to suggest that the basal ganglia form a likely origin for swearing, in concert with the nearby emotional centres in the brain – the limbic system. Overall, the close links between swearing and deep-lying brain structures associated with emotion, together with the evidence that swearing appears to be handled away from the brain's usual language centres, indicate that swearing is, neurobiologically speaking, very much connected with emotion.

So a hidden benefit of swearing is that it can provide an extra register of emotional expression. You can choose to swear in order to gain an additional level of language that can really communicate and share the depth of emotion you are feeling. Next to real-life examples this makes good sense. From the negative outburst of Ernest Hemingway's 'The first draft of anything is shit' to the positive of Bryony Shaw's 'I'm so fucking happy!', swearing communicates a depth of feeling in its own unique manner, that is surer to register with the listener than if a sentence free from swearing had been chosen. But, you might ask, if that's the case then why doesn't everyone swear all the time? The answer is because there's an etiquette to swearing which, though it changes constantly, remains ever present. To show you what I mean, let's go back in time to the early decades of the 20th century.

Fined for not giving a damn

A long time ago, lurking at the back of a forgotten cupboard, I found an ancient copy of William Thackeray's *Vanity Fair*. At numerous points in the book the word '*d___*' appeared. It struck me as remarkable that in 1900, when this edition of the book was published, *damn* was an unprintable word. At that time, this now commonplace and very mild swear word was rude! In terms of equivalence, given that novels now publish swear words in full, this rates the *damn* of the early 20th century as more offensive than *fuck* is today. Back in 1900 etiquette demanded that *damn* was used sparingly. However, people could not resist the urge to use it to spice up their communications and so, as time moved on, it became used more often. Eventually, through use, it lost most of its power to be replaced by stronger expressions. But *damn* had it for quite a while.

Clark Gable, as Rhett Butler, famously spoke the line: 'Frankly, my dear, I don't give a damn' in the 1939 film *Gone with the Wind*. At that time the word *damn* was still censored as profane by Hollywood's Production Code Commission (otherwise known as the Hays Code), leading to the film's producer having to pay a US$5,000 fine (which was a lot of money in those days). But this was a loss that the film company was willing to take in exchange for the maelstrom of attention that it anticipated the line would create. And it did, probably exceeding expectations. Indeed, as recently as 2005 the line was voted first in the American Film Institute's all-time top 100 movie quotations in American cinema. As well as providing an excellent example of the power of swearing, the line was also the starting point for psychologists from Northern Illinois University who were interested in whether swearing can influence people's perception of the credibility and persuasiveness of a speaker [*see* Scherer & Sagarin, below].

The researchers reasoned that attitudes had changed so much towards swearing since the 1930s that it might now be possible for a speaker to garner credibility and mount a more convincing argument in the eyes of onlookers by swearing to emphasize a point. The question here then is whether a hidden benefit of swearing might be as a tool of persuasion. The researchers had some student volunteers watch a five-minute video in which a speaker discussed the lowering of college tuition fees. Sometimes the speaker used the very mild swear word, *damn*, at the beginning or end of a sentence, e.g. 'Damn it, I think lowering tuition [fees] is a great idea'. Other times the swear word was omitted: 'I think lowering tuition [fees] is a great idea.' The volunteers in each condition were asked to rate the credibility of the speaker, the intensity of the argument and their attitudes towards the lowering of tuition fees.

The study found that swearing led to more firmly expressed attitudes in favour of lowering tuition fees compared with not swearing. Swearing also led to increased ratings of the intensity of the speech, but there was no effect of swearing on the rating of the credibility of the speaker. These findings show that swearing to emphasize a point can bolster the persuasiveness of your argument. It works by increasing the perceived intensity of your message but does not alter your credibility as a speaker. So a hidden benefit of swearing is that it can make you more persuasive. However, you should use this technique sparingly.

The statement that the student volunteers were rating in the study (the reduction of college tuition fees) was one that they would have already been very sympathetic towards. On the other hand, two previous studies had failed to demonstrate a persuasion effect of swearing, but these prior studies used topics that were not so obviously palatable to the audience. In that case, swearing provided a reason that the observers could latch onto to justify their disagreement. So swearing can be a good way to bolster an argument but only for an audience that is already sympathetic.

This persuasion effect is most likely connected with the emotional punch that swearing packs. But as well as affecting how you can influence others, some different research shows that you can influence yourself beneficially by swearing. Actually, it was my own research that found this.

The ice bucket challenge

In 2004 my second daughter was born and, aspiring to be a modern dad, I stayed with and supported my wife through the labour. After a while it became clear that things were not going according to plan. This was mainly because our daughter was trying, unsuccessfully, to come out feet first. What followed was a very long and difficult labour for my wife, and towards the end her pain was such that she swore out loud. Indeed, she produced a rather impressive selection of expletives during each wave of agonizing contractions. But as the contractions passed and the pain subsided, she became embarrassed and apologetic over having let fly in front of the nurses, midwives and doctors, only to redouble her efforts when the next wave of contractions struck. The staff, however, had clearly seen all of this before. A midwife explained to us that swearing, four-letter words, cursing, profanity, bad language – whatever you care to call it – is a completely normal and routine part of the process of giving birth. Amid the joy at the arrival of our healthy daughter and the mental disorientation of a very difficult and emotional day, I found this fascinating.

When I eventually returned to my desk at Keele University School of Psychology I wondered why it was that people swear in response to pain. Was it a coping mechanism, an outlet for frustration, or what? I did some literature searching to find out what psychologists thought of the link between swearing and pain. To my surprise I couldn't find anything written on this topic so instead I discussed it with my colleagues. Two psychological explanations of why people might swear when in pain were put forward.

The 'disinhibition' explanation was the idea that in the momentary stress of acute pain we enter a state of social disinhibition (a diminished concern for social propriety) and reduced self-control so that words and ideas that we would usually suppress are expressed. The other explanation was that swearing in response to pain represents 'pain catastrophizing' behaviour. Pain catastrophizing is an exaggerated negative 'mental set' brought to bear during the experience of pain. Catastrophic thinking exaggerates the level of threat posed by a painful event and heightens the pain intensity experienced. While there was some plausibility to the idea of swearing being an expression of pain catastrophizing, it also seemed illogical. Swearing as catastrophizing would serve to increase feelings of hurt and discomfort, whereas most people seek to reduce the pain they are feeling.

Over the next few years my students and I at Keele University worked up a laboratory procedure for assessing swearing as a response to pain. We used a forerunner of the briefly fashionable ice bucket charity challenge. Ice water is very useful because it is a stimulus that is painful but not harmful. Known formally as the 'cold pressor paradigm', participants were asked to hold their hand in ice water for as long as they could tolerate, to a maximum of 5 minutes. While doing this we needed them to swear and we thought it important that they used swear words of their own choosing. Initially we had them read a passage of text and they filled in blanks with either swear words or neutral words. Later on we just asked them to provide a swear word they might use if they banged their head or hit their thumb with a hammer, and then we asked them to repeat that during the cold water immersion. The words most popularly chosen were as you would expect: *fuck* and *shit*.

In our first published paper we showed that people withstood the ice-cold water challenge for longer, rated it as less painful, and showed a greater increase in heart rate when repeating a swear word throughout the procedure, as opposed to repeating a neutral word [*see* Stephens, Atkins & Kingston, below]. We thought, based on the rise in heart rate with swearing, that participants were experiencing an emotional reaction to swearing, setting off the fight or flight response, in turn producing what's known as 'stress-induced analgesia'. This is pain relief that makes up one part of the fight or flight response.

In our second paper we again found that swearing led to withstanding the ice-cold water challenge for longer, rating it as less painful, and showing a greater increase in heart rate [*see* Stephens & Umland, below]. It was a great relief to repeat the findings of the first study. Scientists call this 'replication', and obtaining the same findings in a second study is an important part of the scientific process because it underlines that the findings are genuine.

The second study additionally showed that the reduction in pain from swearing was moderated by daily swearing frequency. Let me explain this point further. In this second study we additionally asked people to estimate how often they swear in everyday life. The responses we got ranged from 0 to 60 swear words per day. Interestingly, the higher the daily swearing frequency the less was the benefit for pain tolerance when swearing, compared with not swearing. This suggests that people become used to swearing so that it has a lesser impact the more you do it (or to use its technical name, people become **habituated** to swearing). On the strength of these findings, the sensible advice is not to swear overmuch in everyday situations so that the impact of swearing can be at its fullest when needed most!

In our third paper we aimed to investigate how an emotional response can lead to increased pain tolerance [see Stephens & Allsop, below]. We began with the assumption that the emotion that speakers feel when they swear is aggression. Then we assessed whether increasing aggression alters the experience of pain. In this study we had volunteers play a first-person shooter video game. They played for ten minutes, exploring a virtual environment encountering and shooting and killing a variety of enemies on the way. It worked a treat because afterwards they reported feeling more aggressive compared with the control condition of playing a golf video game. We went on to show that volunteers withstood the ice water challenge for longer and their heart rate remained elevated after playing the first-person shooter game compared with the golf game. This is consistent with our theory that swearing acts on pain perception via the emotion of aggression.

So, our research shows that swearing can help you to better tolerate pain, that too much swearing in everyday situations can reduce its effectiveness, and that swearing probably works by making people feel more aggressive, in turn setting off the fight or flight response. Swearing as a response to pain appears not to be an expression of pain catastrophizing, because if it were, there should have been a heightened sensation of pain with swearing. The idea of swearing in response to pain as disinhibitory behaviour also seems unlikely as this predicts no alteration in pain perception, contrary to our findings. Our research instead indicates that swearing as a response to pain represents a form of pain management. A hidden benefit of swearing is that it can help you to withstand pain.

While this had never been demonstrated in research before, it seems nevertheless to have been very well known in the real world by nurses, midwives and mothers-to-be. Indeed, since the research came out several online dictionaries have included a new word: *lalochezia*, meaning 'the use of vulgar or foul language to relieve stress or pain'. So if you are in a lot of pain but without immediate recourse to medical intervention, then a hidden benefit of swearing is that its pain relieving properties can get you through those first few moments of agony. Once you get to the hospital, however, it's probably best not to swear – it doesn't sit well with medical etiquette. In fact swearing in the clinic is so rare that when it does happen it's worth paying attention to it.

A cry for help

Imagine you are a psychologist working in a dementia screening clinic. One quick way to assess clients for cognitive problems (i.e. when a person's thinking and decision-making are no longer as quick or reliable as they used to be) is to use a test I described earlier that asks very simply for the person being tested to say (or write down) as many words as they can think of beginning with certain letters of the alphabet. A common version uses, for no particular reason, the letters F, A and S, which is why it is known among psychologists as the FAS Test.

So, there you are in the clinic with your client, and the test is about to commence. The client smiles politely as they listen to your instructions and when the clock starts they try and think of words starting with F. There is a short silence and then a word that meets those criteria is put forward: *fuck*. And then after a short while, another: *fart*. But, as the minute draws to a close, no other words are forthcoming. This actually happened at a clinic in the Mary S. Easton Center for Alzheimer's Disease Research at the University of California in Los Angeles. The researcher and clinician conducting the test had the wherewithal to wonder at this unusual patient response and ask the question – can profanity help diagnose dementia? [*See* Ringman et al, below.]

Dementias are diseases of the brain that usually affect older people. They often start with memory problems but go on to affect other mental abilities. There are many different kinds of dementia, for example, Alzheimer's disease, vascular dementia, Lewy body dementia and frontotemporal dementia. While dementia is not a curable condition, some treatments can help, but there are different treatments depending on the type of dementia. Therefore, it is important to be able to diagnose correctly which particular type of dementia is affecting a patient. Unfortunately, correct diagnosis is often impossible until after the patient has died, allowing the brain to be cut open and examined in an autopsy, which is rather late if you wanted to apply some therapy!

One particular type of dementia known as **frontotemporal dementia** is caused by degeneration of the frontal lobes of the brain. Among other things the frontal lobes prevent us from acting on impulses that would contravene social norms. Because of this, the UCLA researchers reasoned that it would not be at all surprising for a patient with frontotemporal dementia to produce swear words in the FAS test. On the other hand, you would NOT expect to hear swear word responses from individuals with Alzheimer's, where the pattern of brain damage is more widespread. Is it possible that swearing can be used to diagnose which type of dementia a patient has?

The study the researchers carried out was very simple. They looked back through their records of FAS test scores for all dementia cases with suspected frontotemporal dementia, and all cases with a clinician's diagnosis of Alzheimer's. The overall test results showed that each group produced similar numbers of words beginning with the letters F, A and S (about five to nine words per letter, on average). However, frontotemporal dementia patients were significantly more likely to produce the word *fuck*, with six of them producing it (19 per cent), compared with none of the Alzheimer's patients. Some frontotemporal dementia patients also produced the words *ass* and *shit*, and, again, none of the Alzheimer's patients produced these swear words.

The fact that some of the fronto-temporal dementia patients produced the word *fuck* but none of the Alzheimer's patients did, indicates that production of the word *fuck* is '**pathognomonic**' for frontotemporal dementia. 'Pathognomonic' means 'characteristic for a particular disease'. The reason for the swearing responses reflects both a reduced concern for social propriety and impaired verbal abilities, both of which are associated with the frontal lobe impairment that is characteristic of frontotemporal dementia. However, given that more than 80 per cent of the frontotemporal dementia patients did NOT produce the word *fuck*, it would not make sense to base diagnosis of frontotemporal dementia on patients saying swear words on the FAS test. This is because while some would be noticed, the majority that do not give swear words would be missed.

Still this research points to another hidden benefit of swearing – to a small extent it can help to diagnose one kind of dementia over another and perhaps enable earlier treatment. It's fascinating that something as simple and everyday as swearing can reveal so much about a person, to the extent that it can indicate one kind of brain damage over another. Of course, dementia is very sad in all circumstances, but it must be particularly hard to watch a close relative succumb to frontotemporal dementia and perhaps start to swear inappropriately and quite out of character. In providing context and information this research may offer comfort to patients' family members and friends.

As an aside, throughout the published paper in which the research was written up, no actual swear words are printed, rather we see *f*ck*, **ss* and *sh*t*. This seems a little prudish for a piece of science writing published as recently as 2010. *The Guardian* newspaper has printed swear words in full for some years now, and it can only be a matter of time before all swear words are published in full in all sources. Interestingly, the research paper does reproduce the words *fag* and *fart* in full, which must have been down to editorial judgement. Of course, judgement is something that must always be carefully exercised in the context of swearing if you are to extract maximum effect with minimum upset. In fact, as the final section in this chapter will demonstrate, it is all about the context when trying to understand how swearing is understood and received.

Unavoidable swearing

We all know that swearing is rude. So, if someone came up to you and said: *fuck it, fuck you and get your fucking legs out of here* you'd be rightly miffed. Well, actually, not necessarily. The thing with swearing is that it is very much contextual. What's fine in one set of circumstances isn't fine in another. For example, in a survey of UK television viewers asking what kinds of swearing they find acceptable on TV, swearing in response to pain or in response to unexpected or surprising news was acceptable to most people. On the other hand, using swear words in anger against someone or using swear words throughout speech almost without noticing was generally unacceptable. But, believe it or not, there are situations in which swearing can demonstrate politeness and a thoughtful taking into

FIGURE 3.2 Production workers packing detergent

consideration of the feelings of others. To exemplify this we must head 'down under' to a New Zealand soap factory where we will meet a longstanding group of co-workers with a strong sense of group identity.

One team of soap packers at what was then the Lever Rexona plant in Petone, near Wellington, New Zealand, went by the nickname 'The Power Rangers'. They were a close-knit group of 20 mostly male co-workers. Now, these workers were like many company employees the world over and liked nothing more than having a good whinge about their bosses, co-workers from other departments and each other. More than 35 hours of recordings of everyday, factory floor conversations were made by researchers from Victoria University of Wellington [*see* Daly et al, below]. Something very interesting quickly became apparent. When talking with each other, the Power Rangers' cursing and swearing was unsurpassable. Here's an example: one worker complained he was bored of working on one particular production process by saying *'fucking sick of this line'* to which his colleague replied *'(the other line is) fucking worse'*. And another: two colleagues have a moan about the time it takes for overtime monies to be paid, one saying *'fuck man I got short pay last week again'* to which the other responds, jokingly, *'stick it up your fucking arse you did overtime you cunt'*. And a third: two female colleagues gossip about a co-worker, with one saying: *'that dumb mole that did my laminating… dumb bitch… where the fuck's all that stuff'*.

The interesting thing about these exchanges is that they were good natured – nobody was upset and the words were spoken evenly and in good humour. In this context, among these long-term work partners, the use of expletives that could otherwise be considered highly offensive was instead used to indicate close relationships and camaraderie between team members. However, when the Power Rangers were recorded having conversations with non-Power Rangers from elsewhere in the factory, even though they were of equal status in the organization, there was no swearing at all.

Swearing in this context serves as a solidarity symbol – these people knew themselves to be on such good personal terms that they could swear at each other with impunity. As the researchers say, the negative emotional strength of swearing is, in this context, converted into a positive attribute; *fuck* signifies the co-workers saying 'I know you so well I can be this rude in front of you'. And really, it's no great surprise to hear that language can be this nuanced and fluid. That's why these days when you hear someone describing something as sick or wicked you know that its state of health or evilness are not at question. Word meanings change and fluctuate depending on the context and swearing is no different.

And it goes beyond the factory floor. Within the military, on sports pitches and in sports changing (locker) rooms the use of swearing to promote a sense of group identity is rife. In fact, we had a plumber round while I was writing this chapter and we were discussing the New Zealand soap workers study. Our plumber immediately identified with the scenario. He told me that he had been to three jobs by himself that morning and hadn't sworn once, but he knew that at the next job there would be several members of his company there and, as he put it, 'the swearing will be unavoidable'.

So another hidden benefit of swearing is that it can reinforce close bonds between people. Swearing, far from being rude and alienating, can be a shared code and a sign of belonging. You might notice yourself that there are some social situations in which you never swear and others where you do. Probably without even realizing it, what you are doing in those latter situations is using 'industrial language' to forge social bonds.

Wrapping it up

Comprehensive studies of public swearing indicate that it comprises 0.3 per cent to 0.7 per cent of speakers' daily verbal output. Assuming an average of 15,000–16,000 words spoken in a day the average speaker uses 60–90 offensive words per day and the overwhelming majority of these are conversational rather than harmful. Researchers at MCLA have recorded several thousand public episodes of swearing and have conducted numerous interviews about swearing in laboratory settings and none has resulted in physical aggression or complaints from the people taking part. The MCLA researchers' conclusion from all of this seems reasonable: swearing leads to no obvious social harm [*see* Jay, below]. This may seem quite a radical statement but it's a view that is becoming shared by the Establishment.

Recently in the UK, British judge of the Court of Appeal of England and Wales, Sir David Michael Bean, ruled that police officers were unlikely to feel harassed or distressed when members of the public swear [*see* Wardrop, below]. The ruling centred on a case in which a young man swore within earshot of police who were subjecting him to a drugs-related stop and search. The ruling was based on the high frequency with which the four-letter words are used and heard in everyday life and, crucially, because the young man did not swear directly at the police, but rather the way he swore reflected his own frustration (e.g. '*Fuck this man. I ain't been smoking nothing.*'). Clearly there is a societal debate to be had on when it is and is not acceptable to swear but swearing is no longer the universal bad that it once was.

Swearing conveys emotion like no other words do, and as this chapter shows, there are numerous hidden benefits of swearing. At first blush swearing may seem a frivolous research topic for a psychologist to pursue. But if one considers that psychology is the study of the minds of people, and if one agrees that people are emotional beings (more Captain Kirk than Mr Spock), then understanding swearing, as the language of emotion, can improve our understanding of psychology.

In his book *Blue streak: Swearing, free speech and sexual harassment* the comedian Richard Dooling makes an excellent point when he says that the four-letter words are 'inextricably bound up with almost everything' [*see* Dooling, below]. A rather gruesome website records the final utterances of fatal air-crash pilots, captured on the black box flight recorder [*see* www. planecrashinfo.com/lastwords.htm]. In those fleeting moments before death, the level of stress and emotion is immense and, of course, swearing is common. The website records the words, but I won't here because they lose their gravity out of context. Nevertheless, these sad final words emphasize a very important hidden benefit of swearing: from birthing mothers with brand-new babies to the last few moments of precious existence, swearing is, quite literally, the language of life and death.

Further reading

Allan, K. & Burridge, K. (2009), 'Swearing', in *Comparative Studies in Australian and New Zealand English: Grammar and Beyond*, eds Pam Peters, Peter Collins, Adam Smith (John Benjamins, Amsterdam), pp 361–86

Bowers, J. S. & Pleydell-Pearce, C.W. (2011), 'Swearing, Euphemisms, and Linguistic Relativity', *PLOS ONE* Vol. 6 Issue 7

Daly, N., Holmes, J., Newton, J. & Stubbe, M. (2004), 'Expletives as solidarity signals in FTAs on the factory floor', *Journal of Pragmatics*, Vol. 36 pp 945–64

Dooling, Richard, *Blue streak: Swearing, free speech and sexual harassment* (Random House, New York, 1996)

Hughes, Geoffrey, *Swearing: A Social History of Foul Language, Oaths and Profanity in English*. 2nd Revised Edition. (Penguin, London, 1998)

Jay, T. (2009), 'Do offensive words harm people?', *Psychology, Public Policy, and Law*, Vol. 15 Issue 2 pp 81–101

Jay, T., Caldwell-Harris, C. & King, K. (2008), 'Recalling taboo and nontaboo words', *American Journal of Psychology*, Vol. 121 No. 1 pp 83–103

Jay, K. L. & Jay, T. B. (2015), 'Taboo word fluency and knowledge of slurs and general pejoratives: Deconstructing the poverty-of-vocabulary myth', *Language Sciences*.

LaBar, K. S. & Phelps, E. A. (1998), 'Arousal-mediated memory consolidation: Role of the medial temporal lobe in humans', *Psychological Science*, Vol. 9 No. 6 pp 490–3

McEnery, A. & Xiao, Z. (2004), 'Swearing in modern British English: the case of *fuck* in the BNC', *Language and Literature*, Vol. 13 Issue 3 pp 235–68

Ringman, J. M., Kwon, E., Flores, D. L., Rotko, C., Mendez, M. F. & Lu, P. (2010), 'The Use of Profanity During Letter Fluency Tasks in Frontotemporal Dementia and Alzheimer's Disease', *Cognitive & Behavioral Neurology*, Vol. 23 Issue 3 pp 159–64

Ross, H. E. (1960), 'Patterns of Swearing', *Discovery*, Vol. 21 pp 479–81

Scherer, C. R. & Sagarin, B. J. (2006), 'Indecent influence: The positive effects of obscenity on persuasion', *Social Influence*, Vol. 1 Issue 2 pp 138–46

Stephens, R. & Allsop, C. (2012), 'Does state aggression increase pain tolerance?', *Psychological Reports*, Vol. 111 Issue 1 pp 311–21

Stephens, R., Atkins, J. & Kingston, A. (2009), 'Swearing as a response to pain', *NeuroReport*, Vol. 20 Issue 12 pp 1056–60

Stephens, R. & Umland, C. (2011), 'Swearing as a response to pain – effect of daily swearing frequency', *Journal of Pain*, Vol. 12 Issue 12 pp 1274–81

Telegraph, The Daily (2008), 'Bryony Shaw prompts BBC apology by swearing after Olympic windsurfing bronze', *The Daily Telegraph*, 20 Aug 2008. Downloaded 10 February 2012 from: www.telegraph.co.uk/sport/olympics/2589960/Bryony-Shaw-prompts-BBC-apology-by-swearing-after-Olympic-windsurfing-bronze.html

Wardrop, M. (2011), 'Swearing at police is not a crime, judge rules', *The Daily Telegraph*, 21 Nov 2011. Downloaded 3 February 2012 from: www.telegraph.co.uk/news/uknews/law-and-order/8902770/Swearing-at-police-is-not-a-crime-judge-rules.html

Van Lancker, D. & Cummings, J. L. (1999), 'Expletives: neurolinguistic and neurobehavioral perspectives on swearing', *Brain Research Reviews*, Vol. 31 pp 83–104

4
Floor it

Car chases and stunts have been a mainstay throughout cinema history. In the silent movie era audiences chortled when, in the 1920 film *Get Out and Get Under*, Harold Lloyd leaped from the moving car he was driving to retrieve a dropped suitcase, before comically running to give chase to the still-moving but now driverless automobile. Later in the same film Lloyd shakes off pursuing police motorcyclists in one of the earliest screen examples of the deliberately misplaced Road Closed sign. Sent the wrong way, the hapless cops tumble from their machines as they career off the end of an unfinished section of roadway.

A more gritty realism became apparent in the car-chase genre towards the end of the black-and-white period. Robert Mitchum's 1958 movie *Thunder Road* portrays grim-faced law enforcement officers giving chase to scowling illegal liquor runners in classic American fast cars of the era, such as the Ford Fairlane. But the real coming of age of the cinema car chase was the iconic pursuit scene from the 1968 film *Bullitt*, in which cop Steve McQueen guns his Ford Mustang GT 390 muscle car over the crests and dips of San Francisco's steep hills in pursuit of the bad guys' mean-looking Dodge Charger R/T.

Subtler portrayals of fast cars and driving can be found beyond the cinema. The idea of speeding as a mild personality flaw is well illustrated in Colin Dexter's *Inspector Morse* detective novels. The portrayal of the main character, Morse, as a man who likes his beer and enjoys a series of liaisons with female characters, is counterpointed by his sidekick, the happily married Sergeant Lewis. While eschewing drinking, womanizing

FIGURE 4.1 Steve McQueen in *Bullitt*

and late nights, Lewis admits to one weakness – speedy driving on the A roads and motorways around Oxford.

But there's an issue here – how can we reconcile the undoubted popularity of speedy cars and fast driving with its darker side encapsulated by the slogan from road safety campaigns around the world, including ROSPA's (Royal Society for the Prevention of Accidents) a decade ago in the UK, that 'speed kills'? [*See* ROSPA, below.] This chapter explores fast driving as told within the pages of psychology research papers, seeking to establish whether there are hidden psychological benefits of 'flooring it'. To begin, let's return to Colin Dexter's speedaholic Sergeant Lewis. Maybe you or somebody you know shares such a weakness. A fascinating piece of psychology research can very quickly reveal your driving style.

What kind of driver are you?

Imagine you are driving along a 60 mph (100 km/h) trunk road. With that speed limit it's likely to be fairly straight without sharp bends. It's a nice day, there are some other vehicles around but it's not congested and you're making good progress. Maybe you have the radio on or some music playing. Perhaps you are chatting to a friend or family member sharing the car with you. As you pass under one of many bridges spanning the road I want you to freeze the action and survey the scene in front of you – the view under the bridge, the windscreen, the inside of the car, your own body. Now – what are you doing with your hands? Do you have both hands on the steering wheel? Maybe one hand is on the gear stick or draped out of the open window. I want you to record how you are holding the steering wheel. If two-handed, express how you are holding the wheel as a clock time, such as ten to two, quarter to three or whatever. If one-handed, just note the hour on the clock face where your one hand is gripping the steering wheel.

You are wondering why I asked you to do this. Did I mention there were some people standing on the bridge? Researchers from the University of Canterbury New Zealand were watching as you passed beneath them [see Fourie et al, below]. They have done this many times before and have published several research papers on how your driving style is linked to the position and number of hands that you place on the steering wheel. In their most recent study they watched more than 2,000 vehicles drive by. As well as the number and position of hands on the steering wheel they collected information on whether the driver was a man or woman, their speed measured using a radar gun and the distance between their vehicle and the one in front of them.

What did they find? Well, thankfully most people (80 per cent) had at least one hand on the visible top half of the steering wheel. But only a quarter of drivers were holding the wheel with both hands. Most of the drivers observed were driving one handed – or at least they had only one hand on the visible part of the steering wheel. This is interesting because the usual advice to learner drivers is to place the hands at the ten-to-two position, in which case both hands would be visible.

Drivers who did have two hands visible on the top part of the steering wheel were twice as likely to be female, and drove slightly slower on average (69 kp/h) compared with one or no-handers (70 kp/h). The scientists on the bridge also observed that drivers with two hands visible drove slightly further behind the car in front, at an average of 60 m, compared with those with one or no hands visible, who followed at an average of 52 m.

The novice scientist might be tempted to conclude, because they occur together, that hand position directly influences speed and following distance. However, just because things happen at the same time does not mean that one must have caused the other. This is another example of a correlational finding similar to the link between moderate drinking and improved health discussed in Chapter 2. This research does not tell us that hand position causes risky driving, or vice versa. But it does show that hand position indicates risky driving.

So if you tell me how you hold your steering wheel, I'll tell you what kind of driver you are. The quarter-to-three, ten-to-two or five-to-one positions indicate that you drive slower and leave a greater safety margin in terms of the distance between your car and the one in front. If that's how you saw yourself the instant you passed under the bridge, then congratulations. You are a safer driver. Any other configuration including one or no-handed driving, well, I think you get the picture.

But if you are tempted to speed, you are in good company. In fact there is something of a vice in the United Kingdom for driving over the posted speed limit. Another survey in which traffic scientists stood at the roadside, which I shall return to later, found that in certain 30 mph zones, 47 per cent of vehicles observed were over the limit [*see* Taylor et al, below]. We might reflect on the popularity of rapidly propelled cars in popular fiction and in real life – what is it that makes speeding attractive? If psychology research is to shed any light on the allure of fast driving then studies of drivers convicted of speeding are a good place to begin looking.

Who d'you think you are – Nigel Mansell?

While it might not sound very scientific, simply asking people about their opinions and behaviours is a straightforward and commonly used approach available to psychology researchers. Precisely this approach was used by British scientists from the University of East Anglia. They examined questionnaire responses from 464 UK motorists who had been caught speeding [*see* Blincoe et al, below]. Each driver was asked to explain how the speeding that led to their conviction came about.

Most of the convicted motorists were male and, as you might expect, the reasons offered varied. Some drivers were greatly upset by their speeding ticket. As one driver said:

'Whoever has the job of placing the cameras should be ★★★★★★ shot!'

Some said it was accidental and they had mistakenly believed the limit to be higher. This was a particular problem on roads with varying speed limits. One driver bemoaned:

'I was caught speeding on a road where the speed limit changes from 30 to 40 mph and it was an honest mistake. I was doing 39 on what I thought was a 40 mph part of the road.'

Other drivers reported that they deliberately drove above the speed limit because they considered it to be too low based on the weather, visibility, the absence of pedestrians and the superior technical capabilities of modern vehicles. One driver put it very succinctly:

'The concept that "speed kills" put out by the police, government and others is a complete and utter fallacy that has no valid scientific proof. Careless and dangerous driving can kill, speed in itself does not.'

That speeding is sometimes by accident but other times a deliberate act is useful in our quest to understand the benefits of fast driving. The second quote is particularly illuminating as it demonstrates the absence of any mental link between increased speed and increased risk of crashing, completely underplaying how dangerous a car crash can be. And car crashes can be very dangerous indeed.

The Formula 1 driver and the clinical psychologist

In 1962 the British racing driver Stirling Moss was taking part in the 100-mile Glover Trophy race at the Goodwood racing circuit near Chichester, southern England. Enjoying his best spell as a driver, he easily qualified first to start the race in pole position, ahead of the other competitors. However, once the race began things began to unravel. A mechanical problem with the gears forced a pit stop that saw him lose the lead to another British racing legend, Graham Hill. Moss rejoined the race two laps behind Hill but determined to fight back. Striving to catch up, Moss and Hill went side by side into the 120-mph left-hand bend known as 'St Mary's'. Hill appears to have been unaware that he had been caught and drove the usual racing line, which consequently squeezed Moss off the edge of the track. Once on the grass, the slippery surface rendered the brakes and steering useless in altering the path that the car was following. After skidding along for some way, Moss's Walker Lotus 18/21 single-seat racing car ploughed into a grassy bank exploding in a ball of flames, smoke and debris.

Moss had fractures to the leg, arm, cheekbone and eye socket (pictured), but the worse effects of the rapid deceleration of the impact caused the right hand side of his brain to detach from

FIGURE 4.2   Stirling Moss following his 1962 crash

the skull. This is serious because blood seeping out of the torn blood vessels can accumulate between layers of tissue to cause a haematoma. As the volume of blood grows it can crush the soft brain tissue causing permanent damage. The haematoma that Moss suffered put him in a coma for 38 days.

As well as providing a stark illustration of the dangers of fast driving, there is a fascinating psychology research story attached to Stirling Moss's case because Berenice Krikler, the clinical psychologist at the Atkinson Morley Hospital in London who treated Moss, wrote up her assessment of his injuries in a research paper [*see* Krikler below].

Krikler was called upon to determine, psychologically, whether and how much Moss had recovered from his brain injuries during his rehabilitation. The usual way of doing this would be for the psychologist to run some standard tests of mental abilities like memory, reaction speed, hand-eye coordination and so on, and to compare the scores of the patient with 'normal' scores already compiled by the test developers. It occurred to Krikler that elite racing drivers were likely to be substantially different to the general population on whom the normal scores were based. That being the case, the usual comparisons would be meaningless in relation to Stirling Moss. A solution was quickly found. Krikler invited a small group of elite motor racing drivers of the time, Moss's friends and rivals, to provide a more realistic set of normal scores against which to judge Stirling Moss's injuries.

According to Moss's authorized biography [*see* Edwards, below], Krikler's racing driver group consisted of Innes Ireland, Graham Hill, Bruce McLaren, Roy Salvadori and Jack Brabham. In today's terms this would be like calling upon Fernando Alonso, Lewis Hamilton, Kimi Räikkönen, Sebastian Vettel and Jenson Button. Each driver was asked to complete a number of tests of mental abilities. Comparing their scores with the published normal scores provides some fascinating insights into the psychological make-up of top-level racing drivers.

The drivers had an average of 122 IQ points, revealing that they were high above the normal intelligence quotient of 100 IQ points, and in fact were among the top 10 per cent most intelligent people. Despite this, the drivers were no better than the average person on a task of hand-eye coordination requiring using a stylus to follow a marked out curved path without crossing over the edges. The drivers did, however, show a greater awareness of making mistakes than is usual. On a task requiring the production of the correct letter to continue a sequence (e.g. A, C, E, G, __), the drivers were below average when working at their own pace, but above average when asked to go quickly. An early forerunner of a driving simulator called the Miles Trainer was also used. This was an electronically operated device with a screen showing a moving image of a road to be steered along, and from time to time a buzzer sounded requiring immediate response by pressing buttons with the hands or feet. The racing drivers reacted to the buzzer quickest when they were driving the simulator at a faster pace, whereas members of the public reacted quickest when driving the simulator at normal road speeds.

Overall, the five elite racing drivers were found to be highly intelligent, to have fast reactions (particularly when under stress) and to have good concentration, control and judgement. The injured Moss, on the other hand, performed quite poorly on these tasks and particularly tracing a path with a stylus. Stirling Moss more or less fully recovered from his injuries – but he never drove competitively again. Moss is quoted as saying that his car control, which previously had been a matter of reflex, instinct and intuition, was now only possible with effortful concentration. Where before he drove 'automatically', he now had to think his way around a circuit, making him feel less in control. A frustrated Stirling Moss quit racing in 1962 at the age of 32.

The details and aftermath of Stirling Moss's career-ending crash vividly demonstrate how dangerous fast driving (or rather, fast stopping) can be. You might expect, given the history of race drivers that have been killed on track, including greats like Jim Clark, Gilles Villeneuve and Ayrton Senna, that everyday drivers would be very wary of the risks of fast driving. And yet they seem not to be – why might this be? Perhaps it's because racing driving is so far removed from road driving in terms of the types of car, the use of safety equipment and the absence of speed limits on the race track. Maybe racing driving and road driving are so unlike as to be incomparable. Actually, some psychology research evidence for this is provided by a study in which psychologists got almost literally behind a racing driver's visor.

Staying on the black stuff

This research was based on the idea that racing drivers on a familiar circuit don't need to use vision in the same way as normal road drivers. Whereas regular road drivers use vision to perceive the direction of the road and important features such as traffic lights or junctions, racing drivers, having already learned a track, use vision only to update their knowledge of the placement of their own vehicle on the circuit. This was the theory, anyhow. To test it a group of researchers studied the eye movements made by the Formula 3 racing driver Tomas Scheckter as he lapped the Mallory Park racing circuit in Leicestershire [*see* Land & Tatler, below]. The researchers set up a system with two cameras. One was mounted on the driver's helmet looking ahead, and the other was focused through his visor to film his eye movements. These were linked by a computer programmed to be able to record where in his field view the racing driver was looking as he sped around the track.

As was suspected, the researchers found that the driver relied remarkably little on vision to navigate the racing circuit at high speed. Unlike a road driver he didn't focus on features of the road such as the kerbs or corner apexes (the apex is the midway point along the inside of a bend) but instead fixed his vision as far along the track as was possible to see. This makes sense because, driving from memory, race drivers need only to update where on the circuit they are at any given time, so as to be able to know what inputs (steering, braking or accelerating) are required. It makes sense for a race driver to focus as far ahead as they can so that there is as much notice as possible of any obstacle or problem ahead.

The only exception to this pattern was on a hairpin bend (a very sharp bend shaped like a 'U') when the driver looked rapidly from left to right as he approached. Actually this is an example of an often-used technique in circuit racing – picking a physical trackside marker, such as a fence or shrub, and judging the moment of braking relative to it. This helps the driver to brake optimally; neither too early, wasting valuable time, nor too late and risking skidding beyond the turning-in point. Even today's Formula 1 drivers make use of this technique – if you look closely you will see trackside signs counting down 300 m, 200 m and 100 m on the approach to each bend.

This study provides a clear illustration, if one were needed, of how much race driving is removed from normal road driving. The difference is such that it makes no sense for road drivers to base judgements of the risks of fast driving on public roads from observations of race drivers lapping circuits. This partly explains how it is that road drivers lack insight into the link between faster driving and greater risk. However, this lack of insight is further fuelled by the tendency for drivers to overestimate their own level of driving skill. It turns out that drivers, even very good drivers, are notoriously poor at judging their own driving ability.

On the road

In the 1970s, the idea that some drivers have better car control than others led to lobbying in the US for a 'super-driver' licence for exceptionally skilled drivers. One of the benefits would be reduced insurance premiums for this group of elite, assumed to be low-risk drivers. The key phrase here is 'assumed'. Is there a group of exceptionally skilled, super-safe drivers who should qualify for such benefits? A good test of whether advanced motorists really are safer would be to examine the public highway driving records of people who have already trained and practised to develop an above-average driving skill-set. Researchers set about doing exactly this, but to begin they needed to identify a group of skilled drivers and car enthusiasts. The group they settled upon was made up of 447, mostly male, racing driver members of the Sports Car Club of America from Florida, New York and Texas. The drivers gave permission for their on-road driving records to be obtained for the study. This enabled the researchers to compare the race drivers' public-road crash history, speeding fines and other violations over the previous five years with a comparison group of non-racers [*see* Williams & O'Neill, below].

Intriguingly, rather than finding a reduced level of traffic violations in the more highly trained and presumably more competent race driver group, the opposite was true. The race drivers had more than double the rate of speeding fines and increased rates of crashes and other violations compared with the non-racers. This clearly contradicted the starting position for the research – that there exists a superior class of driver who, thanks to a deep interest in cars and driving, develops superior skills that manifest as safer driving. It seems that, on the contrary, while being a racing driver probably does reflect superior driving ability and car control, these skills are not deployed to the benefit of safer road driving and, in fact, race drivers were more likely to transgress road laws and become involved in accidents.

Of course, this is now a 40-year-old study and you might question whether today's racing drivers take road safety more seriously. There's been no updated version of the study so one cannot say for sure. Still this research shows that being a technically good driver is not the same as being a safe driver, and there is no reason to suppose that this would have changed.

Even among a group of highly skilled car enthusiasts there appeared to be a lack of appreciation of the link between speed and safety. So what about speed as a risk factor in normal road driving? Earlier I described a study in which motorists caught speeding went on record expressing, in no uncertain terms, the opinion that driving over the speed limit does not itself pose a safety risk. But is that true?

We know where you live

To investigate the relationship between speed and crashing, researchers from the Transport Research Laboratory, a UK road research organization, stood at the roadside armed with radar guns and notepads [see Taylor et al, below]. They recorded the registration numbers and speed of a great many passing cars. Later, the addresses of the car owners were obtained from the UK Driver and Vehicle Licensing Agency (DVLA) and each owner was sent a questionnaire asking who was driving and how many crashes they had been involved in.

More than 10,000 motorists responded. They had been in an average of one crash every four years since learning to drive. Comparing the speed driven through the radar trap with the number of crashes was very revealing. For every 1 per cent increase in speed there was a 13 per cent increase in the number of crashes for motorways, and an 8 per cent increase in crashes off the motorway. To put this into everyday terms, if the average speed on a section of motorway was 70 mph, a driver travelling at 72 mph would have not one crash every four years, as was the average, but one crash every three years. This would add up to a sizeable number of extra crashes over a 50-year driving career. That the risk of crashing can be so astonishingly increased by such a modest increase in speed certainly adds a great deal of perspective to the research I talked about earlier showing that people driving with one or no hands visible on the steering wheel drive on average at 1 kp/h faster than those with two hands visible on the steering wheel.

On the other hand, before we get too carried away I should point out that this is another example of two things happening together similar to the steering wheel/hand position study described at the start of this chapter. Just because speedier drivers have more crashes, it does not necessarily follow that excessive speed causes crashes. It could be that drivers who are careless crash more often AND tend not to adhere to the speed limit. So, this research is not proof that an increase in speed causes an increase in crashing. But given what we know about crashes it seems quite likely that speed would, at least in part, cause crashes.

If you think about it, crashes usually occur not from one simple cause but from what you might call a series of unfortunate events. For instance, on a motorway one driver might change lanes without checking their blind spot – the area adjacent to their shoulder that they cannot see without swivelling their head and which is beyond the area covered by the wing mirror. This usually would not cause a crash because, in all likelihood, there would not be another car overtaking at that precise moment. Even if there did happen to be a car overtaking, the driver in the next lane would usually be able to take evasive action. But what if the other driver had, at the same moment, glanced away from the road to check their sat nav screen? Adding excessive speed into that scenario, a crash becomes more likely because it cuts down the available time in which either driver can react.

Overall then, research points to a link between faster driving and reduced safety. So how can it be that many drivers are so blissfully unaware that this is the case? The answer lies in how driving is experienced on a day-to-day level. Because crashing is a rare occurrence (car trips almost never involve crashing), making a mental link between driving faster and an increased risk of crashing does not occur to most drivers. Without such a link the way is clear for drivers to drive quickly because… Well, why? I guess not appreciating (or under-estimating) the risks involved is part of an explanation for the allure of fast driving, but it isn't an explanation on its own. Risk is only one half of a cost-benefit trade off. We still haven't tackled the other half, which is what people perceive as the benefits of fast driving. Let's turn now to psychologist Graham Hole and his book *The Psychology of Driving*, in which he makes an interesting suggestion [*see* Hole, below].

Thrills not spills

The tendency some people have to particularly enjoy varied, novel and intense experiences is known to psychologists as 'sensation-seeking'. It is usually discussed in the context of the degree of risk that somebody is willing to accept in the pursuit of such experiences. Sensation-seekers are typically drawn to activities like rock climbing, scuba diving, hang-gliding or parachute jumping. Research has found that, among other things, sensation-seekers get greater enjoyment from a thrilling experience, are less willing to tolerate boredom and don't tend to hold back as much as others [*see* Roberti, below].

As Graham Hole argues, sensation-seeking holds promise as an explanation for the attraction of fast driving. For one thing, men tend to have higher sensation-seeking tendencies compared with women, and men also tend to drive faster than women (as was the case in the survey of drivers caught speeding mentioned earlier, most of whom were male). In addition, research shows that there is a relationship between having sensation-seeking tendencies and carrying out risky driving manoeuvres like speeding. On the other hand, the relationship just mentioned is actually rather modest – one study of high school students showed that sensation-seekers were more likely than non-sensation-seekers to drive at more than 80 mph. However, this finding was somewhat eclipsed by the revelation that, actually, the vast majority of the students interviewed (80 per cent) admitted to having driven at over 80 mph. The reality is that fast driving is widespread and by no means confined to sensation-seekers.

So, although sensation-seeking seems on the face of it to provide an explanation for the attractiveness of fast driving, many people who choose to drive fast are not sensation-seekers at all. This leads Graham Hole to conclude that sensation-seeking only partly explains risky driving and speeding. I am inclined to agree, and in fact to go a step further in dismissing sensation-seeking as rather a hollow explanation for the attraction of fast driving. Sensation-seeking does not answer the question of why fast driving provides a thrill or sensation worth pursuing.

There is a great emphasis on the enjoyment of speed in combination with driving skills within 'car culture', for example, in car enthusiast magazines or TV shows such as the internationally syndicated series *Top Gear*. And yet none of the psychology research studies that I have so far talked about have mentioned fun in the context of fast driving. Perhaps considering the psychology of enjoyment can help us to understand the attractiveness of fast driving.

Mihaly Csikszentmihalyi (pronounced "Mee-hy Cheek-sent-mee-hy") developed the influential **Flow Theory** of the psychology of enjoyment [*see* Csikszentmihalyi & LeFevre, below]. He based his ideas on psychological research using 'experience sampling'. This involves volunteers carrying around electronic devices that can be set to beep at certain times over the course of a day, or several days and nights. The volunteers are asked to write down details of whatever they are doing and thinking when the beeper sounds. The information gathered allows researchers literally to sample people's experiences and consequently to make connections between what people were doing and how they were feeling at the time.

According to Flow Theory the feeling of enjoyment is a combination of novelty and accomplishment in overcoming a challenge [*see* Csikszentmihalyi, below]. The point about the degree of challenge is important. For an activity to be enjoyable there must be a good, although not a certain chance of completing it successfully. Under these conditions 'flow' is the feeling you get when you become so immersed and absorbed in an activity that you forget all other concerns. During flow, you are challenged and yet confident that you will succeed. It is a state of high involvement and enjoyment during which time seems to pass very quickly. Interestingly, Csikszentmihalyi's research volunteers often reported experiencing the sensation of flow if they happened to be driving when their electronic 'experience sampling' beeper sounded [*see* Csikszentmihalyi & LeFevre, below].

But there is driving and driving, and some driving moments are undeniably more enjoyable than others. I would suggest that city driving in congested traffic with continuous hold-ups can be tedious. Added to this, long journeys along featureless, unchanging roads can bore drivers to the point of distraction – actually, self-distraction, in the form of daydreaming.

A boring journey

The pop psychology notion of being 'lost in a daydream', as sung about by the 1960s band The Lovin' Spoonful, raises an intriguing question around whether it is ok to drift off into reverie behind the wheel. By what means psychologists might go about researching this is not obvious at first. How can you get people to daydream to order and how could you measure that while they are driving? In fact, this was no problem for researchers at the University of Illinois – they used their fully immersive high-fidelity driving simulator [*see* He et al, below]. This consisted of a real car, housed in a laboratory, with computer-controlled steering wheel and pedals, surrounded by a 360-degree screen on which computer-generated roads and scenery were projected. I have used a simulator much like this at the UK road research organization Transport Research Laboratory. It is uncannily like driving a real car.

To prompt daydreaming, volunteer drivers were asked to undertake a deliberately boring simulated car journey. The roads were straight and there was never any oncoming traffic. There was a car up ahead with the instruction to drive at a safe distance behind. A following vehicle was added to encourage regular mirror checks. The only relief from the tedium was the occasional simulated crosswind. This setting was ideal and soon after setting off the drivers began to daydream. Whenever they became aware of this happening they were asked to press a button on the steering wheel. Each driver had, on average, 5.7 daydreaming episodes during the one-hour journey, or roughly one daydream every ten minutes. As you might expect, this was slightly reduced during crosswinds.

To see whether daydreaming affected car control, driving performance in a nine-second window just before each button press was compared with driving performance in a nine-second window just after each button press. Interestingly, daydreaming didn't affect the average speed, the following distance to the car in front, how well the car was driven in lane (not veering from edge to edge but staying in the centre) or how far up or down the road that the drivers chose to look. But during a daydream the drivers tended to stay fixed at one speed whereas it is more usual to make numerous small adjustments, correcting for either slowing down or speeding up relative to the traffic around them. Also, most importantly, daydreaming drivers tended more often to look straight ahead rather than checking their side mirrors.

The conclusion from the study was that daydreaming while driving poses a slight safety risk. The tendency to look straight ahead while daydreaming means that drivers do not scan or monitor the road environment around them as much as when they are not daydreaming. This shows that a daydreaming driver is less aware of the other vehicles around them on the road, which could contribute to increased risk of crashing. This is useful to know, because it provides a concrete suggestion as to what should be the first thing we do when we snap out of a driving daydream – check your mirrors!

Of course, driving a simulator is not the same as driving a real car on the road. The knowledge that one is not really driving and so could crash without damage or injury must alter the driving task in subtle ways. On the other hand, driving a simulator can be a very immersive experience. Once while driving the simulator I reached the end of the computer-generated environment and had the very unnerving experience of driving off the end of the road into a vast white nothingness. I stopped, opened the door and stood looking back watching as simulated cars and lorries thundered towards me until, at the point where the road ended and the white void began, they simply vanished into thin air.

Motorcyclists of Taiwan

The realization that driving can sometimes be engaging but at other times be a bore brings us closer to understanding the hidden benefit of flooring it. A particularly relevant aspect of Flow Theory is the relationship between enjoyment and challenge. As the degree of challenge in any situation gets lower, so feelings of flow (enjoyment) decrease also. But this carries an important implication – if an activity becomes less enjoyable, then it is possible to ramp up the enjoyment by increasing the degree of challenge. Perhaps speeding is the expression of ramping up the degree of challenge during everyday driving. At faster speeds the driver is more challenged because they must respond to the road environment with greater urgency. Maybe the hidden benefits of fast driving arise because of the greater risk and challenge that it presents. A study carried out in Taiwan points towards exactly that [*see* Chen & Chen, below].

Researchers asked 277, mainly male riders of 'heavy motor-cycles' (as opposed to scooters or mopeds) a series of questions about how they rode and what they thought about riding. The study specifically included questions arising from Flow Theory about the degree of challenge and enjoyment of riding a motorcycle, such as: 'I have fun riding a heavy motorcycle', as well as questions about intentions and experiences of going over the speed limit, such as: 'When riding a heavy motorcycle, I intend to speed, if possible.' They also asked questions around attitudes towards speeding and sensation-seeking.

Interestingly, of all the questions asked, the answers that best explained speeding were challenge and enjoyment. Those riders that rated challenge and fun highly were also more likely to say that they would ride over the speed limit. This was particularly the case for high sensation seekers. This confirms the idea that when driving conditions are perceived as unchallenging, speeding is an expression of boredom, or rather people floor it as an antidote to boredom. At least that seems to be the case for high sensation seekers.

Journey's end

This chapter has talked about the attraction of fast driving in fiction and in real life and has looked in detail at several pieces of psychology research that help provide a scientific explanation of what underlies that attraction – what the benefits of 'flooring it' might be. We saw that some people caught speeding did so accidentally but others deliberately exceeded the limit. We followed Stirling Moss's crash and recovery under the care of a clinical psychologist. From behind the visor of a speeding racing driver it became apparent that road and racing driving are very different activities. We found out that driving safety is not related to driving skill (over and above basic competence) and that safety is reduced at faster speeds. You found out what kind of driver you are by virtue of how you hold the steering wheel, and some practical advice – that checking mirrors is a good idea when you snap out of a daydream behind the wheel – was offered.

In trying to understand the benefits of fast driving, sensation-seeking was rejected as a hollow explanation because it only leads to a further question of why it is that speeding is a sensation worth seeking. The psychology of enjoyment, and specifically Flow Theory, illustrates how, for some people, speeding seems to be a way of overcoming boredom by increasing the level of challenge arising from the driving task.

The attraction to fast driving seems to arise because of a combination of a lack of appreciation of how the risk of crashing increases if you drive faster, combined with some drivers' tendencies to use speed to make mundane driving more interesting and enjoyable. This has implications. Improving drivers' common knowledge on how speed affects crashing together with finding other ways to make driving more interesting could reduce speeding on public roads, so improving public safety without diminishing driver enjoyment. The challenge lies in thinking up new and safe ways of making everyday driving more interesting and challenging.

Further reading

Blincoe, K. M., Jones, A. P, Sauerzapf, V. & Haynes, R. (2006), 'Speeding drivers' attitudes and perceptions of speed cameras in rural England', *Accident Analysis and Prevention*, Vol. 38 pp 371–8

Chen, C. F. & Chen, C.W. (2011), 'Speeding for fun? Exploring the speeding behavior of riders of heavy motorcycles using the theory of planned behavior and psychological flow theory', *Accident Analysis and Prevention*, Vol. 43 pp 983–90

Csikszentmihalyi, M. & LeFevre, J. (1989), 'Optimal experience in work and leisure', *Journal of Personality and Social Psychology*, Vol. 56 Issue 5 pp 815–22

Csikszentmihalyi, Mihaly, *Flow: The Psychology of Happiness: The Classic Work on How to Achieve Happiness*, (Rider, London, 2002)

Edwards, Robert, *Stirling Moss: The Authorised Biography* (Orion, London, 2001)

Fourie, M., Walton, D. & Thomas, J. A. (2011), 'Naturalistic observation of drivers' hands, speed and headway', *Transportation Research* Part F, Vol. 14 pp 413–21

He, J., Becic, E., Lee, Y. C. & McCarley, J. S. (2011), 'Mind Wandering Behind the Wheel: Performance and Oculomotor Correlates', *Human Factors*, Vol. 53 Issue 1 pp 13–21

Hole, Graham J., *The Psychology of Driving* (Lawrence Erlbaum Associates, New Jersey, 2007)

Krikler, B. (1965), 'A preliminary psychological assessment of the skills of motor racing drivers', *The British Journal of Psychiatry*, Vol. 111 Issue 471 pp 192–4

Land, M. F. & Tatler, B. W. (2001), 'Steering with the head: The visual strategy of a racing driver', *Current Biology*, Vol. 11 Issue 15 pp 1215–20

Roberti, J. W. (2004), 'A review of behavioral and biological correlates of sensation seeking', *Journal of Research in Personality*, Vol. 38 pp 256–79

ROSPA. 'A history of road safety campaigns'. Downloaded 2 February 2015 from: www.rospa.com/rospaweb/docs/advice-services/road-safety/history-road-safety-campaigns.pdf

Taylor, M. C., Lynam, D. A. & Baruya, A. (2000), 'The effects of drivers' speed on the frequency of road accidents', *TRL Report* 421. Bracknell: Transport Research Laboratory

Williams, A. F. & O'Neill, B. (1974), 'On-the-road driving records of licensed race drivers', *Accident Analysis & Prevention*, Vol 6 pp 263–70

5

Fancy that

Do you have a favourite song? Are the lyrics about love or romantic relationships? Chances are if you answered 'yes' to the first of these questions, then you'd have followed up with a 'yes' to the second – because stories around love remain an enduring subject matter in song lyrics. In fact from the 60s to the 80s 'love' was the most influential theme in the music charts. It lost some ground in the 90s when it dropped to being popular music's third most influential theme and the slip continued into the 'noughties' when it was down to ninth place. But that's still the top ten and a demonstration that love endures in today's popular music. But it's not in quite the way you might think. Say you could get a computer to analyse the lyrics of every hit song between 1960 and 2009. Would you expect upbeat or downbeat songs to most often feature the word 'love'?

Some advertising scientists from North Carolina State University have already carried out just such a computerized analysis of the 10,556 words contained in the 956 number one songs over those five decades [see Henard & Rossetti, below]. But while 'love' was among the most influential words, it tended more often to be in songs about loss rather than aspiration. Think Del Shannon's July 1961 number one hit 'Runaway' ('I'm a-walkin' in the rain/Tears are fallin' and I feel the pain') or, more recently, JLS's 2009 number one hit 'Everybody In Love' ('When they're gone you don't know how to go on').

You might say that pop music is not the greatest barometer of human emotion but I would disagree. So would advertisers. They recognize the importance of emotion in developing messages that resonate on a deep level with consumers – and get them to buy more stuff. People who make commercials place great value on popular music of all genres because it brings results. Music can slow the rate at which people get bored of an advert, known technically as 'wear-out', and reduce how quickly an advert is forgotten. That's why it was advertisers that commissioned the research into pop lyrics I just mentioned. But is it true – can romantic love really be more of a downer than an upper?

Physically, intense romantic love can bring about heart palpitations, trembling, loss of appetite and other symptoms of heightened emotional arousal, including feelings of a sexual nature. Intense romantic love can also generate upbeat feelings of euphoria. However, there is an almost obsessive element to love, which includes an incessant thinking about and craving to be with the person that is the focus of the love. This means that when being with the object of one's desire isn't possible, love can also produce feelings of profound frustration.

Researching pop music lyrics tells us that romantic love is more of a liability than a pleasure. In song lyric terms love is more 'Achy Breaky Heart' than 'I Want to Hold Your Hand'. And it's this darker, more obsessive side that will be the focus of this chapter as we explore the science of romantic love – and find out that it isn't all it's cracked up to be. Contrary to what you might think, romantic love can actually be quite bad for you.

Love and cigarettes

By adulthood most people will have experienced the heady rush of romantic love – the state of longing for union with another. We are able to estimate how widespread love is thanks to some anthropologists from the Universities of Nevada and Tulane, who made a detailed analysis of the writings of 166 different human societies from all over the world [*see* Jankowiak & Fischer, below]. The cultures ranged from hunter-gatherer societies in the Kalahari desert in southern Africa to the Yanomami village dwellers of the Amazon rainforest, and from Arctic animal herders to Chinese citizens of the Song Dynasty in AD 1000. Clear indications of the existence of love in those cultures included phrases like 'hearts on fire', 'amorous nature' and 'prolonged love-despair'. They found that 88 per cent of the cultures whose documents they assessed contained at least one example confirming romantic love. For the cultures not included in this total it was a case of absence of evidence rather than contradictory evidence because there were no examples of cultures actively preventing or outlawing individuals from experiencing romantic affection. This research indicates that love occurs in cultures worldwide, such that it is a defining aspect of what it is to be human.

Given how widespread love is it is quite appropriate that psychology and other branches of science concerned with human behaviour have begun to carry out scientific research into love. In the 1970s the psychologist Dorothy Tennov coined the word 'limerence' to describe the feelings of intense romantic love in her book *Love and Limerence: The Experience of Being in Love*. It hasn't really caught on much in popular speech – probably because it has no semantic derivation; 'limer' is no more than a pleasant-sounding, but otherwise arbitrary pairing of syllables.

One approach to studying romantic love in a scientific way is, very simply, to ask people who are in love to report their feelings. The 'Passionate Love Scale' is a questionnaire developed by psychologists in the 1980s for just this purpose [*see* Hatfield & Sprecher, below]. It consists of 30 questions about romantic love including: 'I have an endless appetite for affection from _____'; 'I melt when looking deeply into _____'s eyes'; and 'I would feel despair if _____ left me'. (NB insert the name of your beloved at '_____'). Participants rate each question according to whether they consider it not at all true, moderately true or definitely true. Despite its low-tech nature the questionnaire has proven to be a useful tool over the years. Psychologists from the University of Central Florida used the Passionate Love Scale to assess how American men and women of different ages experience romantic love [*see* Wang & Nguyen, below]. The researchers were surprised to find that, contrary to expectations, romantic love occurred with a similar intensity in men and women across all adult ages.

You might think people falling in love regardless of age and culture is a beautiful state of affairs. But I would have to disagree. Smokers argue paradoxically that their habit is one of the pleasures that makes life worth living, while at the same time it wipes years off their life expectancy. Love represents a similar mental doublethink – making life worth living but, as popular music lyrics attest, at the same time being unbearable. You are probably beginning to doubt my sanity in comparing love with cigarettes. But you don't have to take my word for it that love is best avoided. The science of love can speak for itself on that issue – starting with scientific research demonstrating that what we call love may be no more than an illusion.

Two stooges short

In the early 1960s psychologists from Columbia University in New York [*see* Schachter & Singer, below] gave a group of research volunteers an adrenaline injection – but they lied about what it was. The volunteers were told it was a vitamin called Suproxin, but in fact this was a made-up name. They were informed that the purpose of the injection was to see how it would affect their vision, but this was also untrue. Shortly after the needle had been planted into their upper arms, and the plunger dropped, the adrenaline (also known as epinephrine) would have begun pumping around the volunteers' arteries and veins and their bodies would have begun to react. The substance would have caused their blood pressure and heart rate to increase, they would have begun to shake a little, their cheeks would have started getting hot and they would have found themselves need-ing to take shorter, more rapid breaths than usual. The volunteers would have been well aware of these physical changes in their bodies and most likely wondering what on earth was going on.

At this point, in pairs, the volunteers were shown to a room and asked to fill out questionnaires. However, soon after they had begun, one volunteer in each pair began to act very strangely. Sometimes he clowned about, making and throwing paper balls and paper planes, shooting a catapult, and even doing the hula hoop. Other times he got very angry over the questions they were given to answer saying things like 'I'll be damned if I'm filling out number 25' or 'The hell with it! I don't have to tell them this'. I should mention at this point that the second vol-unteer who clowned or got angry was in on the experiment. An insider posing as a regular study volunteer like this is known technically as a 'stooge'. In this case the second individual, the stooge, took great care to avoid giving the game away but they were actually following instructions from the psychologists in charge of the experiment.

So why give people adrenaline and then put them in a room with a clown or a curmudgeon?

The real reason the researchers injected unknowing volun-teers with adrenaline was to look at the interplay between body and mind. Specifically, they wanted to try to get to the bottom of a chicken-and-egg problem concerning human emotion. The question was this: what comes first when we feel emotion – the psychological aspect or the physiological? In other words, when we feel a strong emotional response to something – say a knot of fear in the stomach, sometimes called a 'gut response'– do we first feel fearful mentally and does that set off the gut response, or do we get the gut response first and then interpret that gut response as fear?

The researchers suspected it was the latter. They expected that if you give someone adrenaline without telling them, then when they start to feel the physiological arousal brought about by the adrenaline (but without knowing why it is occurring) they will seek an emotional explanation for that arousal. The researchers thought they could influence how the volunteers would interpret their emotional state by what happened after the adrenaline injection – and they were right. Those volunteers placed with a clown felt cheery and behaved happily (some even joined in making and throwing paper planes). The volunteers sharing a room with the grumpy person became angry themselves.

This experiment shows that, actually, the way we feel emotions is contrary to what you might think. For the chicken-and-egg problem of what comes first in emotion – the psychological feeling or the physiological arousal – this study indicates that the physiological part (gut feeling) comes first and the psychological emotional label (such as happy or angry) is added on. This psychological part is an interpretation based on how the body is responding and what is going on around us. But this is not how people assume their mental life is organized – most would say that the psychological aspect of emotion is paramount. What does it mean for our psychology if our minds are led by our bodies? What does it mean for love? To find out we should pay a visit to a Canadian National Park.

Love and vertigo

The Capilano Canyon in Canada is a sheer sided ravine 137 m across and 70 m deep and through it flows the Capilano River. In the late 19th century some engineers hoisted a couple of steel cables across to support a narrow, single-track footbridge. As very high bridges go this one is particularly terrifying. Its flimsiness and tendencies to tilt, sway and wobble don't augur well considering its great height and huge span. Its low hand rails

FIGURE 5.1 The Capilano Bridge

add to the impression that falling over the side is imminent – and it's a very long way down to the boulders and shallow rapids below. Crossing it is very scary – so terrifying, in fact, that it has become one of the most popular tourist attractions in Vancouver. It was also an ideal location for a pair of Canadian psychologists to stage a fascinating piece of research. [*see* Dutton & Aron, below]

The researchers set up a situation in which men crossing the bridge were approached by a pretty female student on the other side. She explained that she was doing a project on tourist attractions for her psychology class and asked them to fill out a questionnaire. When the volunteers were handing back their completed questionnaires she offered to explain the research in more detail when she had more time. At this point she tore the corner off a sheet of paper, wrote down her name and phone number and suggested they phone her later on. As a point of comparison this procedure was repeated for some other male volunteers crossing a solid wooden bridge with high handrails just 3 m above a small stream. So how many phone calls did the pretty female student receive?

Half of the men spoken to after crossing the scary adrenaline-inducing suspension bridge phoned. But only 12 per cent of the men crossing the low, solid bridge placed a follow-up phone call. In the research world this is a sizeable difference – but how can we explain it? This study was designed to set up a similar situation to the one in which volunteers were unknowingly injected with adrenaline, only this time they received a 'natural' shot of adrenaline due to fear of heights. Also, this time the focus was on emotions around love and romantic attraction rather than happiness and anger, which were the focus of the adrenaline study. But otherwise the two studies are very similar and just as the volunteers given adrenaline misinterpreted the physical arousal brought on by the adrenaline to be the natural emotions of joy or anger, here men misinterpreted the physical arousal brought on by crossing a scary bridge for the natural feelings connected with romantic love.

But if those feelings are more connected with crossing one bridge over another rather than reflecting some deep inter-personal chemistry, then what does that say about this thing we call love? Clear signs of attraction were shown to occur simply because some men misinterpreted their own emotional arousal. In mistaking fear for love these research volunteers have pro-vided a scientific illustration of the illusory nature of love. And this isn't the only means by which illusion can lure us into a sense of false romance.

Law of averages

What makes a person's face attractive? It's an age-old ques-tion that was thought to be too subjective to be worth serious scientific scrutiny until recently. Still, multi-million pound cos-metics and plastic surgery industries demonstrate the huge level of interest in physical attractiveness. Some recent science tells us that attractiveness is not, as you might at first think, linked with distinctiveness; it's actually the opposite.

While having a distinctive look hasn't harmed the career of supermodel Cara Delevingne (pictured), studies of peo-ple's preferences for faces have repeatedly shown that, actually, people are more impressed by averageness. The science back-ing this up has involved the creation of artificial face images built by inputting images of a great many people's faces onto a computer and averaging across their features to produce a sin-gle composite image. In preference trials these highly average faces are consistently rated most attractive [*see* Peskin & Newell, below]. What's more, the bigger the number of faces sampled to build a composite face, the more attractive the composite face is judged to be. So, next time you feel like telling a beau

FIGURE 5.2 Cara Delevingne

how attractive they are, it would be very honest of you to com-
plement them on their averageness. Of course that probably
wouldn't go down too well – honesty is not the best policy in
this case!

As well as averageness there is another important factor
that influences how physically attractive a person's face is perceived to be. It's not symmetry, youthfulness, skin clarity or

skin smoothness. It's something much more mundane and it steamrollers romantic notions of soul mates and fatal attractions. Psychologists from Trinity College Dublin [*see* Peskin & Newell, below] ran a very simple research study. Male and female volunteers looked at a series of smiling female faces. Each time they were shown a face they were asked to rate its attractiveness. Some of the faces they saw just once while others they saw six times. By the end of the study the repeatedly viewed faces were picking up higher attractiveness ratings for no other reason than the duplicated exposure. Did you think familiarity breeds contempt? Not at all – quite the opposite.

This tendency to form a more positive impression due to familiarity is known to psychologists as the '**mere exposure effect**'. It applies to many different situations and not just faces. It's been shown that people will evaluate photographs, sounds, shapes, names and even made-up words more positively if they have encountered them before. One fascinating study by a psychologist from Sheffield Hallam University showed that it even affects the judging on that most hallowed of events, the annual Eurovision Song Contest [*see* Verrier, below].

Eurovision has grown ever more popular with more and more countries wanting to enter. Its expansion led the organizers to introduce a semi-final stage in 2004 organized in such a way that only certain of the newer entrant countries are invited to perform and be judged at this stage. Other more established countries are allowed to omit the semi-final and go straight into the final. This meant that after 2004 some countries in the Eurovision Song Contest final were already familiar to the judges because they had performed in the semi-final, whereas others were not. What's more, an analysis of the judging process of the final found that countries that were in the semi-final received more points than those not previously seen – just because of that extra familiarity.

So another downside of love is that the person who you fall in love with, contrary to what you think, might not necessarily be a super soul mate, or have distinctive looks too stunning to ignore. The attraction could be down to the simple fact of you having seen a particular person regularly! This is because of the general human tendency to favour the familiar. The 1980s band Imagination sang in their UK hit single 'Just an Illusion': 'Follow your emotions anywhere/Is it really magic in the air?'. Magic – no! Science tells us that attraction, the precursor to love, arises due to mere exposure. Which is why love is clearly for dummies.

But why do we attach such importance to love given that it rests on such shaky foundations? Perhaps it's because love is so difficult to pin down that we fall for it – if we ponder for a few moments on what love actually is it's much less clear than you might think. It's certainly true to say that love is closely bound up with emotion. When things are going well in your love life you will feel emotions like joy, affection and expectation. But let's be clear – plenty of different experiences can make us feel those same things. Likewise, when the love rollercoaster dips and we feel negative emotions such as anger, disgust and sadness these too are emotions that you are likely to feel in other situations besides falling in love. Which begs the question – if love isn't a unique emotion, then what is it?

'What is love anyway?'

Finding out what parts of the human brain become activated by love would be one scientific way of bettering our understanding. A good deal is already known about the functions carried out by different structures within the brain so this approach could feasibly answer some quite fundamental questions about the nature of romantic love. It could tell us whether love should best be thought of as an emotion in its own right, or perhaps as a collection of more fundamental emotions. It could also confirm the proposition contained in the title of the 1975 hit single by Roxy Music, 'Love is the drug'. Can it be true – can love be like a drug you can get hooked on?

Some psychologists from the State University of New York at Stony Brook investigated the romantic brain [*see* Aron et al, below]. The first problem the researchers encountered was where to find enough loved-up people to make the study worthwhile. Being based in the population-dense New York City area there was no shortage of volunteers responding to a newspaper advert placed seeking individuals who were intensely in love and in a relationship, despite the hard-nosed reputation of east coast Americans. These volunteers were asked to undergo a functional Magnetic Resonance Imaging (fMRI) brain scan (a type of scan that was described in Chapter 1).

Each volunteer brought two photographs to the research centre – one of their romantic partner and a second photograph of a friend of the same age and sex as their beloved. Then, while having their brain scanned, the volunteers looked at each photograph in turn. This meant that the differences in brain activity while viewing the two different images could be used to identify the parts of the brain that become active in response to intense romantic love, compared with friendship.

Before we get to the findings, which were intriguing, I need to give you a quick primer on some of the structures within the brain and what they do. I want to draw a distinction between the **cortex** and the **subcortical regions**. The cortex, which makes up the corrugated outer surface of the brain, evolved relatively recently and is associated with intellectual activity such as problem solving. On the other hand, the subcortical regions are located deep within the brain and are known to become activated when raw emotions are experienced, such as joy or sorrow. It is generally accepted that the subcortical regions are phylogenetically more ancient – that is, they evolved much earlier than the cortex. It is convenient to talk of the old brain, meaning the subcortical centres that, among other things, are involved with emotion, and the new brain, meaning the cortex, with its involvement in intellectual activity.

The New York study found that when these loved-up volunteers viewed pictures of their beloveds both old and new brain structures became active. New brain structures were most likely to become active for relationships that had been established for a longer time. Parts of the new brain that became active were the frontal and temporal lobes, and this activity most likely reflects ongoing intellectual processes such as memory, familiarity and attention. These processes are necessary if you are to recognize your beloved when you see them – romance would not proceed very far if you were unable to do this. Old brain structures that became active were components of subcortical reward regions such as the **caudate** and the dopaminergic cells of the **ventral midbrain**. These reward pathways have been found to become active in response to stimuli that most people think of being pleasurable, such as sex (discussed in Chapter 1) and drugs (discussed in Chapter 2), as well as eating chocolate or receiving money.

Returning to the question of what love is – these findings are very revealing. Romantic love activated a reward pathway that responds to a variety of pleasurable activities rather than activating a specific 'love' centre in the brain. Rather than thinking of romantic love as a single emotion, it would be more accurate to understand it as a goal-directed emotional state. What does this mean? For one thing, it's much less romantic to view love in this way. When smooching your beloved they probably wouldn't appreciate it if you told them that they set off an intense goal-directed emotional state in you. But it also means that love is not an end in itself but is more like an instruction to behave in a certain way, almost certainly to ensure procreation and species survival. This implies that love isn't spiritual but earthly. What a con!

The finding that romantic love activates the same reward pathways as chocolate, money and cocaine provides a scientific basis to the poetic idea of love being a very potent drug. Bryan Ferry and Roxy Music were right – love does indeed have a great deal in common with narcotics. Perhaps now my earlier analogy comparing romantic love with tobacco seems less far-fetched. But the idea of love being like a drug poses some further questions. In particular, if drugs are renowned for one thing it is their unwanted and sometimes harmful side effects. We know that alcohol will give you a hangover (see Chapter 2), that marijuana will give you the munchies and certain prescription drugs can make you drowsy. So might there be unwanted and unpleasant side effects of this drug-like condition we call love?

Love sick

If I ask you to think about romantic love what do you picture in your mind's eye? Chances are it would be something along the lines of two people holding hands, gazing blissfully into one another's eyes and smiling contentedly. When we think of romantic love it tends to be in an idealized form and most scientific research has also bought into this version of romantic love. Take, for example, the New York study I was just talking about in which lovers gazed at photos of their romantic partners while undergoing a brain scan. The volunteers in that study were specifically requested to think of pleasurable occasions that they had shared with their beloved while the brain scan was carried out. For instance, one volunteer reported thinking about a fondly remembered occasion when she and her lover took a romantic 3 a.m. stroll to a 7-Eleven store. While unconventional, it's easy to appreciate the romance in this.

However, romantic love is not an exclusively pleasant experience. Most people, thinking back to adolescence when love first strikes, can recall how the undeniable pleasures of falling for someone were accompanied by a good deal of insecurity, anxiety, uncertainty and most likely jealousy thrown in for good measure. This reflects the point I made earlier, based on the analysis of pop song lyrics, that love is more downer than upper. Science has attempted to measure the extent to which love can lead to negative as well as positive emotions.

Researchers from the Tehran University of Medical Sciences recruited some student volunteers and, very simply, asked them some questions about their love lives [*see* Bajoghli et al, below]. They asked whether they were in love. If they were, they asked how often they thought about the person they were in love with, how distracting those thoughts were and how easy it was for them to resist the urge to think about the person they loved. Volunteers' levels of depression and anxiety were also measured using the same questionnaires that a psychiatrist might use to diagnose these conditions. Interestingly, the volunteers with higher scores for being in love also had higher scores for depression and anxiety. Should we be surprised by this?

We should not. We've all been through the mill and experienced love sickness, a condition recognized long ago by the philosophers Plato, who called it a 'serious mental disease' and Socrates who labelled it 'madness'. After listening to the volunteers in their study relate their experiences of being in love, the Tehran researchers made the very good point that falling in love requires us to have to deal with not only our own difficult emotions but also those of another basically unknown person. Although obvious, it is insightful to highlight this: that when we fall in love it is usually with a person that we do not know very well. Embarking on a new relationship necessitates the successful negotiation of passion, excitement, commitment, jealousy, risk-taking, self-disclosure and coping with uncertainty. It also requires thinking about shared aims in life, attitudes towards sex, money, peers, family and quite possibly religion as well. This is complicated and demanding and so it is not surprising that new love can take its toll on mental well-being.

Of course, the Tehran research is a survey and so by its nature it is a correlational study. As I first mentioned in Chapter 2, a correlation is a finding that two things occur together – here love and depression – but it doesn't tell us if one caused the other. Love may cause depression, alternatively depression may cause love, or perhaps some third variable causes both. But even acknowledging this the research provides some insights into the darker side of love and flags up the possibility that romantic love may not be conducive to good mental health. As we'll see in the next section, love may not be good for your physical health either.

'Ever Fallen in Love (With Someone You Shouldn't've)'

Love affairs have their own set of problems and unpleasant consequences. Take workplace romances, for example. Scientists have investigated the workplace romance and have even produced a definition: 'a mutually desired relationship involving sexual attraction between two employees of the same organization.' In the UK around 70 per cent of employees have experienced workplace romance, while up to one fifth of us meet our long-term partner at work. This explains how it is that a quarter of office romances lead to marriage. But beware, there are pitfalls of the workplace romance that were nicely outlined in a review paper by a business academic from Glasgow University [see Wilson, below]. The paper highlights how a workplace romance could very well lead to you losing your job – as demonstrated a few years ago by none other than US President Bill Clinton. The consensual sexual relations between a married man and an intern that became known as the Monica Lewinsky affair ultimately resulted in President Clinton's impeachment.

Numerous pitfalls of workplace romances have been reported in the scientific literature. One problem is reduced productivity due to long lunches, missed meetings, late arrivals and early departures. There can also be disharmony among groups of workers due to favouritism, conflicts of interest and flawed or biased decision-making. However, in the interests of balance I should add that these negative effects are not universal and some studies show work productivity rising in individuals in the throes of a workplace romance. Likewise, some workplaces have benefited from increased morale and motivation stimulated by a workplace romance among two popular and well-liked individuals.

Extra-marital love affairs most often generate the biggest amount of negativity among the various players involved. Indeed, if you are a man, science presents a particularly good reason to avoid this kind of love. Health researchers from the University of Florence had access to interview records from more than 1,000 patients attending a men's health clinic. As well as the usual questions that doctors ask about smoking, drinking and illnesses, the men were asked some quite personal questions about their love lives. How would you like it if your doctor asked you 'How many sexual attempts do you have per month?', 'Does your partner have more or less desire to make love than in the past?' or 'Do you have sexual relationships with people other than your usual partner?'. Actually, the patients in these clinics didn't seem to mind too much. Around 8 per cent of those questioned admitted to an ongoing extramarital affair. These men tended to be older, which isn't particularly surprising given that the stereotype of an affair is an older man with a younger woman (e.g. Clinton/Lewinsky) [*see* Fisher et al, below].

Now when you think of that older man/younger woman scenario you have to ask yourself whether this is an altogether wise arrangement. The Italian study showed that men who were having affairs had twice the risk of a heart attack or other major adverse cardiac event. They explained this in terms of the 'extra vigour' accompanying amorous encounters with new rather than established partners. This is consistent with observations in medical research concerning the phenomenon known as **sudden coital death**, which is where a person collapses and dies in the act of sexual intercourse. Though rare, it mostly occurs during extra-marital intercourse outside of the victim's home. This illustrates how having an affair may not only blow your mind, it could also bust a blood vessel with potentially fatal consequences.

But the health risks of love affairs go beyond the physicality – never underestimate the powerful influence of psychology when it comes to health. I mentioned that the Italian men were asked about whether their long-term partners' interest in sex had changed recently. The men were split into two groups – those whose partners were less interested in sex, and those whose long-term partners retained an interest in sex. There was a big difference in the risk for heart attacks between these two groups. In fact, men having an affair whose long-term partners had a reduced interest in sex showed no increased risk of having a heart attack. The increased risk of heart attack in men having affairs was only present for those men whose long-term partners remained sexually interested. It seems that deceiving a sexually available and involved mate produces a profound sense of guilt. It is well-known that psychological concerns contribute to cardiovascular problems, for example prolonged stress is known to increase the risk of having a heart attack. This survey found that men fooling around behind the backs of loving spouses were guilt-tripping themselves into serious health problems.

So avoiding love affairs can save you from getting the sack and, if you are an older married man with a loving spouse, can even save your life. These are undeniable benefits of avoiding fresh romantic love. But what of long-term partnerships? You might think that this will be one area in which love can have a positive effect. But this isn't necessarily the case.

'When I'm 64'

So far I've focused on the early stages of new love. But what happens to love in long-term relationships and is such love beneficial? When they marry, couples vow to spend the rest of their lives together in sickness and in health. It's true to say that the longer the marriage lasts the more these vows get called upon as health declines in later years. Despite what you may think, romantic love can prosper in long-term relationships, although this is likely to be accompanied by compassionate love, which is a friendship-based love involving shared values and long-term commitment. Interestingly, there are some harmful side effects of compassionate love in long-term relationships – but only for men.

Researchers from Auburn University, Alabama, asked married couples in their 60s and older to complete what they called the 'compassionate love task'. This involved asking each partner to 'share a time when you felt your spouse put your needs ahead of their own'. Spouses were asked to describe when this happened, what their spouses did, how it made them feel and if they had told their spouse how it made them feel. Some couples could only muster responses like: 'I don't know the answer to this one'; this example, indicates low compassionate love. On the other hand, one man said: 'She gave up so much to move around the country for my job. It meant everything to me and I am so thankful to her', and this indicated a high level of compassionate love [*see* Rauer et al, below].

Displays of compassionate love in the relationships of older adults had a strangely one-sided effect. Acts of compassionate love by wives to their husbands were associated with better health in wives but poorer health in their husbands. The opposite, however, was not true – acts of compassionate love by husbands towards their wives did not affect either partner. How can we explain this?

The effect may be a consequence of the gender roles that exist in our culture, particularly in the older generations. Generally speaking, women grow up with expectations that they will be good at nurturing and care-giving, and they get to enjoy these kinds of roles during the child-rearing years. Later on in life, women that provide compassionate love to support their husbands reap a benefit from that provision. For the women this seems to be about increasing their feeling of being needed and valuable, which, in turn, enhances their well-being.

On the other hand men in receipt of compassionate love may perceive this as a reminder of their own declining health, perhaps even ushering in a new stage of the marriage in which the wife becomes the carer for the husband. This can exacerbate the husband's fear of becoming a burden on his wife and can erode the husband's feelings of self-competence. This explains how men would react negatively to such care. This can also explain why men do not benefit from providing compassionate love to their wives as, with no gender roles to fulfil, no effect is present. Traditional gender roles can also explain why wives do not feel similarly vulnerable and threatened when their husbands care for them. A traditional female gender role is for a woman to be loved and nurtured by a dominant male. A woman receiving compassionate love from her husband would feel nurtured rather than insecure.

If love in the longer term is detrimental to men, then this adds to the scientific findings I have been discussing in this Chapter, highlighting the pitfalls of love. I've slated love as being a fake emotion likely to arise for the most mundane of reasons with the capability, if not to kill, then at least to seriously harm. But if avoiding love is beneficial, then here's a practical question – can we avoid falling in love by bringing love under conscious control?

A new hobby

I've already mentioned a study in which writings from numerous and diverse human societies were analysed and the vast majority were found to mention love. Indeed, many of the research papers I have discussed in this chapter start off with statements extolling the power and universality of love. These include: 'falling and being in love is a universal behaviour'; 'one of the most powerful and exhilarating states known to humans, namely love'; and 'intense romantic love is a cross-culturally universal phenomenon'. If love is universal then this would suggest strongly that love cannot be brought under conscious control (if it could be then somewhere, some people or societies would have chosen not to fall in love). Unfortunately, this is the closest that science has come towards answering the question of whether we can control love and thereby avoid it if we wanted to. I could not find any research in the scientific literature that answers this question more directly.

Moving beyond science to folk knowledge around love, I did a Google search for 'can love be controlled'. In a TED conversation with the title 'Can you control who you can fall in love with?', one responder replied: 'Yes you can absolutely control who you fall in love with... after the initial attraction'; while another said 'I probably don't give myself over to love, I keep some control'. The general consensus of the discussion was that the first flush of romantic love is beyond control, although we have the capacity to decide whether or not to follow up such feelings, keeping longer-term goals in mind. Remarkably, a series of practical tips for avoiding love can be found on a website called www.wiki.how. The tips include distracting yourself with a new hobby, avoiding flirting and distancing yourself from the person concerned. These don't sound all that convincing to me. So, from this limited sample, folk knowledge concurs with the hints from science – love is uncontrollable and all we can do is try to manage it as best we can.

But if we can't avoid love, then the advice I've been providing in this chapter that love is best avoided is redundant, right? And anyway, love is a central part of what it is to be human so why would anyone want to avoid it, despite its pitfalls? You can't live a totally risk-free life and how we confront and manage risk is what makes life pleasurable and worth living. This is where I must confess that I've been presenting a rather one-sided account so far. In fact, science has uncovered a number of benefits of love that I haven't told you about. In the interests of balance we should talk about these.

The upside of love

If love is a universal human trait then it must be beneficial, and a number of studies have found evidence of this. One benefit of romantic love is that it has an energizing effect. Psychologists from the University of Western Ontario [*see* Stanton et al, below] showed that volunteers in romantic relationships thinking about their feelings for their romantic partner had higher blood glucose levels than when they thought about things they liked to do with a friend that they had no romantic attachment to. These higher blood glucose levels, which gave the volunteers a feeling of being energized, also corresponded with how happy they were feeling.

Staying with research that has examined lovers' blood, being in love has also been shown to be associated with increased levels of a substance found in blood called **nerve growth factor** (NGF). This substance is one of the neurotrophins, which are the molecules that enable neurons (brain cells) to thrive and develop thick networks of connectivity as we grow from children to adults. They also help us to cope with anxiety and other emotions. This increase was discovered by researchers at the University of Pavia in Italy. They recruited volunteers who were 'truly, madly and deeply' in love and in relationships less than six months old. These individuals had higher levels of NGF than volunteers in secure romantic relationships of two and a half years and more, and in volunteers who were single [*see* Emanuele et al, below].

That the difference was due to relationship length shows that only the first flush of romantic love is accompanied by increased levels of NGF. It was a very strong effect, because the greater the degree of romantic love felt, the more raised the levels of NGF were found to be. However, when volunteers still in the same relationship one year later were re-tested, not only had their level of romantic love reduced, but so had their levels of NGF. It was by now at the same level as the single people originally tested. It seems that NGF levels increase during early love, providing the psychological benefit of helping to manage the stress of beginning a new social bond.

One further benefit of romantic love is connected with its setting off of the brain's reward circuits. It seems that romantic love may literally make the world a sweeter place. You may have heard of embodied metaphors such as 'love is sweet' (implying literally that love has a sweet taste), 'sour grapes' (implying that jealousy tastes bitter) and 'being hot-headed' (implying that anger is heat). Psychologists from the National University of Singapore wondered to what extent these metaphors were based on life experience. They carried out an experiment investigating whether feelings of love made people more aware of sweet flavours [*see* Chan et al, below].

They asked some volunteers to write about a time when they felt romantic love and they asked some other volunteers, as a point of comparison, to write about landmarks in Singapore (such as the impressive One Raffles Place skyscraper). Volunteers that had been writing about romantic love rated a sweet and sour candy, a square of bitter Meiji Morinaga chocolate and even plain water as having a sweeter taste. What seems to be happening here is that people may have come to associate love with sweetness because romantic love and eating a pleasant tasting sweet set off the reward circuits in the brain (the same ones I was talking about earlier on).

Perhaps most importantly it has been found that the first stages of romantic love can have a positive impact on long-term relationships (as opposed to some of the problems of compassionate love discussed earlier). In a survey of more than 600 people a psychiatrist from Zurich University Hospital found that marrying one's great love in life leads to a higher level of satisfaction with the relationship than people who did not [*see* Willi, below]. In addition, having *ever* been in love with one's partner led to a higher level of satisfaction with a long-term relationship than if the partner had never been loved. Fascinatingly, love at first sight was just as effective in promoting feelings of satisfaction with the relationship, as did a love taking two months or more to grow. So, despite its pitfalls, a 'truly, madly, deeply' romantic love affair can be an excellent basis on which to base a long-term relationship.

'Love will tear us apart'

I spent most of this chapter highlighting findings from science that would make you think that love is best avoided. For one thing it is easily mistaken (people can't tell it apart from fear); for another, physical attraction for faces, the conduit through which love operates, can be influenced by seemingly irrelevant things like averageness or repetitive exposure. I told you that love is more like an instruction than a unique emotion and how it has more in common with drugs than you might think. A consequence of this is that love may adversely affect your mental health, and not only that, when it comes to physical health love has form as a killer.

However, I later had to acknowledge that, notwithstanding these pitfalls, there are plenty of positives associated with romantic love. I must come clean now – I'm a romantic at heart and would not want to live a life without love. But that doesn't make me at all unusual – on the best evidence we have: love is universal. So to be human is to love and you would have to be crazy to set about consciously and deliberately avoiding love. Of course love goes hand in hand with difficult-to-live-with negative emotions like longing, heartache and jealousy. But it's like anything: you need to experience the lows to properly enjoy the highs.

Mother Teresa provided a unique perspective on the fundamental importance of love when she said: 'There is more hunger for love and appreciation in this world than for bread.' So you should take every opportunity to eat at love's table, even if sometimes what's on offer doesn't go down well. We know that love hurts – that's why we invented pop music.

Further reading

Anon, 'How to Avoid Falling in Love'. Retrieved 4 February 2015 from: www.wikihow.com/Avoid-Falling-in-Love

Aron, A., Fisher, H., Mashek, D. J., Strong, G., Li, H. & Brown, L.L. (2005), 'Reward, Motivation, and Emotion Systems Associated With Early-Stage Intense Romantic Love', *Journal of Neurophysiology*, Vol. 94 Issue 1 pp 327–37

Bajoghli, H., Keshavarzi, Z., Mohammadi, M.-R., Schmidt, N. B., Norton, P. J., Holsboer-Trachsler, E. & Brand, S. (2014), 'I love you more than I can stand! – Romantic love, symptoms of depression and anxiety, and sleep complaints are related among young adults', *International Journal of Psychiatry In Clinical Practice*, Vol. 18 No. 3 pp 169–74

Chan, K. Q., Tong, E. M., Tan, D. H. & Koh, A. H. Q. (2013), 'What do love and jealousy taste like?', *Emotion*, Vol. 13 Issue 6 pp 1142-9

Dutton, D. G. & Aron, A. P. (1974), 'Some evidence for heightened sexual attraction under conditions of high anxiety', *Journal of Personality and Social Psychology*, Vol. 30 No. 4 pp 510–17

Emanuele, E., Politi, P., Bianchi, M., Minoretti, P., Bertona, M. & Geroldi, D. (2006), 'Raised plasma nerve growth factor levels associated with early-stage romantic love', *Psychoneuroendocrinology*, Vol. 31 Issue 3 pp 288–94

Fisher, A. D., Bandini, E., Corona, G., Monami, M., Cameron Smith, M., Melani, C., Balzi, D., Forti, G., Mannucci, E. & Maggi, M. (2012), 'Stable extramarital affairs are breaking the heart', *International Journal of Andrology*, Vol. 35 Issue 1 pp 11–17

Hatfield, E. & Sprecher, S. (1986), 'Measuring passionate love in intimate relationships', *Journal of Adolescence*, Vol. 9 pp 383–410

Henard, D. H. & Rossetti, C. L. (2014), 'All you need is love? Communication insights from pop music's number-one hits', *Journal of Advertising Research*, Vol. 54 No. 2 pp 178–91

Jankowiak, W. R. & Fischer, E. F. (1992), 'A Cross-Cultural Perspective on Romantic Love', *Ethnology*, Vol. 31 No. 2 pp 149–55

Peskin, M. & Newell, F. N. (2004), 'Familiarity breeds attraction: Effects of exposure on the attractiveness of typical and distinctive faces', *Perception*, Vol. 33 Issue 2 pp 147–57

Rauer, A. J., Sabey, A. & Jensen, J. F. (2014), 'Growing old together: Compassionate love and health in older adulthood', *Journal of Social and Personal Relationships*, Vol. 31 No. 5 pp 677–96

Schachter, S. & Singer, J. E. (1962), 'Cognitive, social, and physiological determinants of emotional state', *Psychological Review*, Vol. 69 Issue 5 pp 379–99

Stanton, S. E., Campbell, L. & Loving, T. J. (2014), 'Energized by love: Thinking about romantic relationships increases positive affect and blood glucose levels', *Psychophysiology*, Vol. 51 Issue 10 pp 990-5

Verrier, D. B. (2012), 'Evidence for the influence of the mere-exposure effect on voting in the Eurovision Song Contest', *Judgment and Decision Making*, Vol. 7 No. 5 pp 639–43

Wang, A. Y. & Nguyen, H. T. (1995), 'Passionate love and anxiety: A cross-generational study', *Journal of Social Psychology*, Vol. 135 Issue 4 pp 459–70

Willi, J. (1997), 'The significance of romantic love for marriage', *Family Process*, Vol. 36 Issue 2 pp 171–82

Wilson, F. (2014), 'Romantic relationships at work: Why love can hurt', *International Journal of Management Reviews*, Vol. 17 Issue 1 pp 1–19

6

Stress more

'Suddenly I feel dizzy and extremely nervous. My stomach is convulsing. I know that I am next. I can't seem to look out of the window as the plane makes a sharp right turn. I'm feeling faint. I look out of the plane and contemplate climbing out on to the step. Such contemplation only serves to increase my symptoms. I feel I have turned very pale. The instructor looks at me and genuinely asks if I am OK. I tell him I am, although I know that my response is unconvincing. All I can do is stare at the horizon, and try not to look down. I concentrate on my breathing, slowly inhaling through my nose and out through my mouth. I can feel the instructor checking my parachute, pulling and pushing me back and forth. He then shouts in my ear "I want you to arch your back for Britain, OK?". I nod. Then I hear the instructor shout those dreaded words – "ON THE STEP"' [*see* Hardie-Bick, below].

Several years ago, sitting in my Keele University office I noticed an email advertising a lunchtime seminar. It was a sociology talk and thus out of my area but the title, 'Sky-diving and the Metaphorical Edge' sounded interesting so I went anyway. The talk, by sociology lecturer James Hardie-Bick, described some ethnographic research (Ethnography is the systematic study of people and cultures. It is designed to explore cultural phenomena where the researcher observes society from the point of view of the subject of the study.) carried out at a UK parachuting centre. It made use of the exciting research technique known as 'participant observation'. This is where a scientist conducting a research project intentionally becomes very close to the group under study – so close, in fact, that he or she becomes part of the group and takes part in their activities. In this case it entailed signing up for a parachuting course and making a number of jumps. The opening paragraph of this chapter (above) is the riveting and visceral account of the moments leading up to this sociology lecturer's first static line parachute jump. It clearly induced in him a state of sheer terror – and it makes me wonder why he put himself through all of that in the name of research [*see* Hardie-Bick, below].

So why would a social scientist want to become a parachutist? These days risk is almost always portrayed as having negative consequences. This has meant that everyday activities like drinking alcohol (see Chapter 2) or allowing children to walk to school unaccompanied have come to be viewed as highly risky, even dangerous behaviour. Two silly and over the top examples of this all-encompassing safety culture are banning conkers and snowball fights in school playgrounds. But there's a very interesting paradox in all of this. In a climate where people are portrayed as vulnerable and anxious about falling victim to previously non-existent dangers, why are high-risk activities like parachuting, bungee jumping and fairground rollercoaster rides more popular than ever?

The answer is that these potentially deadly pastimes provide a number of hidden benefits. Actually saying that is rather obvious – if there were not benefits to outweigh the dangers people would not choose to do them. But science (including our parachuting sociologist) has begun to explore the specific benefits of putting yourself into highly stressful situations that not only scare you out of your wits but also, in some cases, present the prospect of your own untimely death. This chapter explores these benefits, starting with a seemingly paradoxical reason why some people choose to leap out of aircraft.

One thousand, two thousand, three thousand, CHECK!

Emotional self-regulation is the idea that people are not at the beck and call of their emotions, but rather they employ various strategies so that they can control their emotional responses when or before they arise. It's said that people who manage to achieve emotional self-regulation have a high level of emotional intelligence. Alternatively, the inability to self-regulate one's emotions is linked with depression and other mental health problems. A predominantly French team of psychologists carried out a survey of women parachutists to try to back up the hunch that some people use the stress of parachuting as a form of emotional self-regulation [*see* Woodman et al, below].

So where did this hunch come from? It all began with a previous study showing that women who take illicit drugs – a high risk activity by most definitions – were more likely than male illicit drug-takers to have the psychological condition **alexithymia**. People with this condition are unable to describe how they are feeling emotionally in words.

Let's do a quick check of whether you have a tendency towards alexithymia. Do you agree or disagree with these statements?

- 'I am often confused about what emotion I am feeling'
- 'I find it hard to describe how I feel about people'
- 'I prefer to just let things happen rather than to understand why they turned out that way'.

An alexithymic person would readily agree with all three statements. When people with alexithymia describe things that have happened to them they will do so with a very flat, monotonic delivery that fails to convey any of the accompanying emotional aspects; you would not be able to discern how the event they are talking about made them feel. The condition is partly a problem with being unable to acknowledge or feel one's emotions and feelings as well as being unable to express them to another person.

The research focused on women parachutists with and without alexithymia and looked at how their feelings of anxiety changed from before a jump to immediately afterwards (within 10 minutes of landing) and then again an hour later. It wasn't a particularly sophisticated piece of research – the researchers just needed to get to an airfield and ask women skydivers to fill out a sheaf of questionnaires.

The first interesting finding was the sheer number of alexithymic women who had taken up parachuting. The researchers estimated that 33 per cent of female skydivers have alexithymia, which was quite high compared with the proportion of women in the general population with the condition, which has been estimated at between 8 and 25 per cent. That more alexithymic women do parachuting provides evidence that women with this condition are drawn to extreme sports for some reason, and more so than women without the condition. However, it was when they examined feelings of anxiety that they could see a clear link between parachute jumping and emotion regulation.

The survey found that women parachutists without alexithymia showed a consistent level of anxiety from before the jump to after landing. Alexithymic women showed higher levels of anxiety overall, but immediately after doing a parachute jump the amount of anxiety they reported feeling was reduced. For these women, who have difficulty in perceiving and communicating their emotions, a parachute jump provides an opportunity first to experience a strong emotion, and then to feel it ebb away.

One hidden benefit of taking part in dangerous sports such as skydiving is that these activities provide a structured outlet for risk-taking. Doing the high-risk activity of a parachute jump allows individuals with a condition affecting the perception and expression of emotion to feel stress and then feel relief from stress. For these people the dangerous activity of parachute jumping presents an opportunity for emotional self-regulation. That's all fine but it's only a small subsection of the population who have alexithymia and who might turn to parachuting as a consequence. So what other types of people feel the need to take up extreme sports? Actually, there is a much more prevalent characteristic that researchers have found to influence participation in stressful and dangerous activities. Here's a clue: other than being famous explorers of one kind or another, what do Sir Walter Raleigh, Robert Falcon Scott and Edwin Eugene Aldrin all have in common?

Who are the danger chasers?

What Sir Walter Raleigh, Scott of the Antarctic and Buzz Aldrin have in common is that they all had older siblings. This means that none of them would have been first in the pecking order when they were growing up. Could it be the case that birth order, in other words whether you happen to be a first born, middle born, last born, or an only child has an impact on your appetite for stress? It's possible, because the parental input received by first-borns, who emerge to novice (first time) parents, is different to that received by later-borns, who emerge to parents who have become well versed in child-rearing matters. These differences in childhood experience could go on to influence attitudes in later life.

Researching birth order became fashionable in the 1960s and 1970s. It was then that a researcher surveyed the male students at the State University of New York at Brockport to see how birth order affects willingness to take part in dangerous sports like skydiving, motorcycle racing, ski jumping and flying.

It was a very straightforward paper-and-pencil type of study and its results were unambiguously clear. The first-born students expressed less willingness to take part in high-risk sports than the later-born students [*see* Yiannakis, below].

This made a later study that did not repeat this finding all the more puzzling. A research group, led by a sociologist from the University of Texas at Arlington, wrote to members of the United States Parachute Association with a number of questions [*see* Seff et al, below]. For a number of dangerous sports, including parachute jumping, hang-gliding and motorcycle racing, they were asked how risky they believed each to be and how often they had taken part in each one. They were also asked whether their main sport, parachuting, was appealing for reasons that emphasized sensation-seeking (so did they agree with statements such as: 'danger is stimulating, even sensual') or reasons that emphasized personal mastery (e.g. 'I learn a little about myself each time I jump'). In this more recent study first-borns did not differ from later-borns in how risky they believed sports like parachuting or motorcycle racing to be; they did not differ in how many times they had participated in these sports; and there was no tendency for first-borns or later-borns to favour either sensation-seeking or personal mastery as motivations for parachute jumping. In short, there were no effects.

So, here we have two studies examining birth order and participation in dangerous sports but their findings do not agree. You might be wondering what happens now – what does science do in situations like this? Actually, inconsistent research findings like this are not unusual for several reasons. For one, the outcomes of science are usually probabilistic. This is particularly true for psychology and the social sciences when we usually declare an effect to be present if a statistical analysis indicates we can be at least 95 per cent sure that it would not happen by chance. Still, this means that 5 per cent of the time

we may falsely declare effects to be present. (NB I have simplified this explanation and would direct the interested reader to
look up 'null hypothesis significance testing' for more information.) Scientists call this the 'error rate', and the fact that
scientists work with an error rate demonstrates that sometimes
(5 per cent of the time) studies will produce misleading results.
The best way to check whether a study's results are reliable is
for a different group of scientists to rerun the same study. This
is called a 'replication'. Quite often one research group finds
something but then another group is unable to reproduce the
finding in their laboratory.

As a scientist I relish the puzzle of inconsistent findings and
enjoy trying to work out how the discrepancy came about.
It's *always* the case that the devil is in the detail. For example, in the above two studies, the first one asked individuals to
rate whether they would be *willing to participate* in a dangerous
sport, whereas the second asked if they had *ever participated* in a
dangerous sport. People tend to put their money where their
mouth is, so I would say that the second study that asked about
actual participation trumps the first study that asked merely
about willingness to participate. So does that mean there's no
effect of birth order on dangerous sport participation?

In this situation my science instincts were telling me that
birth order effects were unlikely because the better study of
the two, the one that used a behavioural measure (how often
have you played dangerous sports) rather than an opinion-
based measure (how willing would you be to play dangerous
sport), found no effect. However, more recently again, researchers from the University of California carried out a review of
all the separate scientific studies they could find on birth and
dangerous sports. A review paper can be described as a 'study
of studies' and is probably the best source of information on
the question of whether birth order affects dangerous sports
participation [*see* Sulloway & Zweigenhaft, below].

Rather than just considering two studies, this review identified 24 different scientific studies looking at birth order and participation in dangerous sports (i.e. participation was assessed rather than merely preference). Averaging across these studies, considering those that showed an effect and those that didn't, the review found an overall positive effect such that later-born children were 1.42 times more likely to participate in dangerous sport than first-borns. This very strong piece of scientific evidence is convincing – it shows that later-borns are more drawn to extreme sports.

The reason why birth order affects the desire to engage in stressful and risky activity is down to family dynamics. First-borns usually enjoy a greater amount of parental attention in the early years because, at this stage of a family, parents do not have to 'dilute' their resources and deal with several children at once. Indeed, research shows that parents pay more attention to first-borns. Not only that but when siblings do come along first-borns are expected to help out with looking after younger brothers and sisters. This means that first-borns become more accustomed to having responsibility and higher expectations placed upon them by their parents compared with younger siblings.

The effect of childrearing on later-borns is to make them more extroverted and open to experience. This is probably because, with an older sibling having already established a useful family role, a younger sibling must think of novel and sometimes unconventional alternative ways to garner parental favour. Linked to this, prior research has shown that willingness to take risks usually has a beneficial pay-off for individuals seeking to improve their social status within groups. This means that younger siblings learn to reap benefits in developing an identity and status within the family by adopting more risky strategies, and they carry forward this successful strategy into the adult world. One outcome of that is a greater preference for dangerous sports than first-borns.

So a hidden benefit of the stress involved in dangerous sports like parachuting is that they can provide an outlet for taking risk in a relatively safe environment for individuals who seek out that kind of excitement. This is effectively what sociologist James Hardie-Bick found in the research that I began this chapter by discussing. The parachutists that he met talked about society becoming overly cautious to the point that modern life had become stifling, with extreme sports being one way of overcoming those cloistered feelings of overprotection. Jumpers talked of how coping with the stress of parachuting was part of the attraction, saying: 'There's something about embracing fear... You just have to live with it. I mean if you didn't have any fear at all then what's the point?'

And be sure that there is plenty of fear and stress involved in jumping out of an aeroplane anywhere from 3,000 to 13,000 feet up in the air with nothing more than a piece of flimsy nylon intervening between precious life and certain death. And it can do strange things to your head.

Freefall recall

'No matter how smart you are on the ground you get stupid the first time you fall out of a plane.' So say parachute instructors the world over. This is the only way they can explain how it is that 11 per cent of parachuting fatalities occur not because of unrecoverable equipment malfunction, but due to human error when a parachutist fails to take timely and appropriate action. Sometimes the main canopy fails, but this does not have to end in disaster because all jumpers have a reserve. However, each year people die unnecessarily because they are unable to martial the mental capacity to recognize the problem and deploy the reserve, resulting in what's known as a 'no pull' with tragic consequences. A group of US psychologists who were also keen amateur parachutists decided to look in more depth at how the extreme stress of a parachute jump can interfere with basic thought processes. They had witnessed how basic mistakes can endanger safety in some of their own classmates at their parachute centre [*see* Thompson et al, below].

One student suffered a panic attack and pulled the cord that severed her attachment to the main canopy even though it had opened properly. Luckily she was in radio contact with ground crew who, with only seconds to spare, guided her successfully to deploy her reserve parachute and survive this potentially life-threatening situation. A second student coming in to land was directed from the ground to steer left but inexplicably pulled hard on his right cord. He ended up crash-landing on the roof of the centre, spraining an ankle in the process. So how is it that otherwise intelligent individuals come to make such basic errors in the air?

The researchers thought it was due to an added difficulty in learning and recalling information in highly stressful conditions. To test this out they thought it would be interesting to get parachutists to carry out a memory test mid-jump. So they recruited some experienced skydivers and kitted them out with a Sony Walkman cassette recorder strapped to the chest (this was in the 1990s – today a digital voice recorder would certainly be used instead). It was arranged that mid-jump, once the main canopy was deployed and the lines confirmed to be free of tangles, the 'play' button would be pressed and a list of words (e.g. 'sandwich'; 'bedroom'; 'spider') would be heard through headphones. Following a short interval, the skydiver had to press the 'record' button and recite as many words as she or he could recall back into the machine. They then pressed 'stop' and got on with the serious matter of steering to the drop zone and getting ready to land. This is a fairly typical way for psychologists to measure memory – apart from the fact that the volunteers taking the test had just fallen from an aeroplane!

They found that memory – recall of the words in the list – was reduced in the air. An average of five words were correctly recalled by the skydivers whereas a second group tested on the ground averaged eight words. Why might recall be poorer during a parachute jump? Several aspects underlie our ability to recall information. Successful memorization requires learning the material in the first place (called 'encoding') and then being able to produce that information from memory when prompted (called 'retrieval'). As a check on whether the disruption to memory occurred at the learning or retrieval stages (or both) the experiment was repeated but with one important difference. This time the parachutists listened to a new word list on the ground and took the recall test in the air (as opposed to doing both parts of the test in the air).

On a second jump, once the parachute had opened successfully and they were gliding through the air, they pressed the 'record' button of the Sony Walkman and recited as many of the new words as they could recall. For these new words that had been learned before ascending to jump no difference was found comparing recall in the air with another group that performed recall on the ground. Overall this shows that the stress evoked by a parachute jump affects the ability to learn new information (encoding) but does not affect the ability to recall information that has already been stored in memory (retrieval).

We can explain this disruption in learning new information under duress as a problem with being able to mentally link the words on the list with the context in which these words were first heard. In this instance 'context' means details such as what jumpers were doing when they first heard the words, what they were looking at as they listened to the tape, how the words made them feel, and any personal memories that the words might have triggered. Normally our memories rely on these additional contextual aspects, known as 'cues' to memory scientists. The reason why the jumpers were unable to make links between the words and the context is simply because the stress of risking life and limb by leaping out of an aircraft blocks the ability to think. We know this thanks to a further study in which skydivers did mental arithmetic problems on the plane shortly before making a jump. They were found to make more errors compared with doing the same tasks on the ground, indicating problems with general thinking ability under stress [*see* Leach & Griffith, below].

So these studies shed light on one aspect of why people become 'stupid' in the air – because the extreme stress of sky-diving interferes with the ability to think, including memory. For a novice skydiver on a first jump it's as if the emotional reaction to the life-threatening challenge of jumping out of a plane overwhelms their normal mental functioning and makes it much harder for them to process information. The stress of a parachute jump makes it harder to perceive and understand the world, making a misunderstanding all the more likely. The consequences can be devastating if they lead to a parachutist cutting away a well-functioning main canopy, or if it prevents them from deploying the reserve chute if the main one failed to open.

But this research runs counter to the theme of the book. There is no benefit to stress if it reduces your ability to understand and interact with the world effectively. Actually, the way that parachute jumping affects our ability to think and reason isn't all negative. A recent study found some beneficial effects in this regard.

A flash in the sky

Where were you when you first heard that Diana, Princess of Wales had died? If you are too young to remember as far back as 1997, can you recall what you were doing when you first heard about the 9/11 attacks? If 2001 is before your time can you remember the circumstances in which you heard about the January 2015 Charlie Hebdo terrorist attack in Paris?

The chances are that if you lived through these iconic news events (and if they meant something to you at the time), then you will be able to remember the circumstances of how you first heard the story. For example, I remember first hearing about 9/11 via a message from my wife on the then new Internet-based MSN Messenger service. I remember sitting in my office (a different one to now) reading a one-line message she had typed saying a plane had crashed into the World Trade Center. I recall at first assuming that a light aircraft must have strayed off course in bad weather. These rich detailed memories for 'big deal' events are known as 'flashbulb' memories because they are very vivid and much clearer than regular memories (e.g. as a comparison I have no idea what my wife and I discussed on MSN Messenger the day before). One of the hallmarks of a flashbulb memory moment is the significant emotional aspect to the event being recalled. I have a personal connection with New York and so, for me, the 9/11 attacks evoked fear, sadness and anger.

Psychologists from the University of California, Davis wondered whether the extreme emotional arousal of skydiving might bolster memory similar to the way that emotion plays an important part in forming flashbulb memories [see Yonelinas et al, below]. They recruited some volunteers who had signed up for a tandem skydive, which involves exiting the plane at high altitude tethered to an instructor (actually strapped onto their back). This kind of jump includes a dramatic freefall lasting up to one minute, covering a vertical distance of around 2 miles, before the parachute is opened and relative calm descends during the gentle drift back to earth. To see how the stress of a tandem skydive affects memory, the volunteers were first shown a series of photographs on a computer. This was one hour before their jump. Then, around two hours after the jump, they were asked to recall as many of the photos as possible by writing short descriptions of them (e.g. 'a man riding a pushbike in a forest'). The experiment ended with a further memory test but this time a recognition test was used. Recognition differs from recall in that rather than having to pluck memories out of the air, so to speak, which is the case for recall, this time they were shown all of the pictures again along with some additional decoy pictures, and they were asked to say, 'yes' or 'no', whether each picture had been shown to them before they did their jump.

Doing the tandem skydive had no impact on how well the volunteers could recall images by writing descriptions. The number of pictures recalled by the skydivers was similar to the number recalled by some other volunteers who waited on the ground instead of doing a jump. However, the skydivers showed better recognition than the volunteers who waited on the ground. Or, at least, the male skydivers did; men who had just done a tandem jump recognized more pictures than men who did not leave the ground. Recognition rates among the women skydivers were the same as those for the women who stayed on the ground, and the same overall as those of the men.

Just to add one further layer of complexity, in recent times memory experts have come to acknowledge two separate aspects to our ability to remember what we have previously encountered. One is called 'recollection' and this is our ability to say with certain knowledge that we have encountered the object previously. An example of recollection would be where we are certain we have encountered an object before because we can remember our reaction to first seeing it (e.g. being excited by it), or we remember where it was that we saw it. The other aspect, 'familiarity', is the feeling that we have previously encountered an object but without being able to provide additional information that would allow us to say that we can recollect it with certainty. The skydive led to higher familiarity scores but had no impact on recollection.

What's going on here psychologically is that, similar to a flashbulb memory, the stress of a tandem skydive enables a memory strengthening process that makes the memories (in this case the photographs) more resistant to the effects of for-getting. In fact, the beneficial effect for familiarity but not rec-ollection (or recall) indicates an overall strengthening of the memory trace itself rather than aspects of the memory retrieval process. The reason why only the men's memories benefited from doing a tandem skydive may be because the men showed a stronger physiological reaction to the skydive than did the women. It seems that women did not find the skydive suffi-ciently stressful to produce the effect.

So a hidden benefit of being stressed is that it can bolster your memory, but this benefit is only apparent after the stress has subsided (two hours later in the skydiving study). So what other mental functions can be improved if we subject ourselves to stress? I've already alluded to the problem in parachuting whereby tragic incidents such as 'no pulls' occur because the jumper isn't able to think through to the correct course of action in time to save their own life. And yet there is a paradox here because one of the most consistently reported sensations people experience during extreme stress is the feeling of life going into a sort of slow motion. A downhill skier who experi-enced time slowing down during a terrifying high-speed wipe-out described it as follows: 'It's like you become hyper-aware, so your perception of time slows down... I remember lifting off and taking forever to hit the ground. I remember thinking – What? I'm still not there yet?' The paradox is this: if time slows down in a life-threatening emergency, then shouldn't people be able to think more clearly under those conditions because, subjectively at least, they have a longer time to think?

Gravity is an awesome thing

The proverb 'Time flies when you are having fun' is a good illustration of the idea that our subjective perception of time can alter. Time is often said to go quickly when we are doing something we enjoy, and seems to drag by very slowly when we are bored. But what about the chilling feeling of time coming to a near-standstill during a life-threatening emergency? Some psychology researchers specialize in how we perceive time. One of the world's leading experts in this field, Professor John Wearden, was until recently a Keele University colleague occupying an office two doors down from me. Perhaps through conversations with John when we occasionally shared lifts I'd long been intrigued by a research paper he'd mentioned describing an experiment investigating this subjective feeling of time slowing down in an emergency.

Of course, it would be unethical to expose people to a real life-threatening emergency for a science project. So researchers from the University of Texas and Baylor College of Medicine had some volunteers do an activity sufficiently scary and stressful to feel life-threatening, without actually being too unsafe [*see* Stetson et al, below]. The chosen activity was a 31-m Suspended Catch Air Device (SCAD) jump installed at the Zero Gravity Thrill Amusement Park in Dallas. A SCAD is a true fall from height in that it comprises a freefall vertical descent without ropes or parachute. Riders are harnessed to a platform during the drop, and the fall is halted only when they come to rest in a giant safety net. Travel writer Max Wooldridge described the moments during a SCAD jump like this: 'There's a tremendous rush of air around me. All of a sudden I am freefalling towards earth, hurtling towards the ground at an alarming 75 mph. Gravity is an awesome thing and I've never known anything that matches this acceleration. Time is suspended and every second feels like 10. There's just enough time to start panicking.'

These research volunteers in Dallas made two SCAD jumps. After the first they were asked to estimate how long their jump had lasted. Like Max Wooldridge, they tended to overestimate the duration of their jump. On average, the jump was estimated to last for 2.96 seconds, whereas the actual freefall duration was timed at 2.49 seconds. This overestimation was consistent with the idea that time passes more slowly during a potentially life-threatening emergency. Think about it: if a given time interval seemed to pass slowly, then you would estimate that it lasted for longer than if it seemed to pass relatively more quickly. Nevertheless, the volunteers' reports of time apparently slowing down were made *after* doing the jump. These were retrospective reports or, in other words, judgements made after the event. The scientists behind the paper wanted to go one step further and find out whether the participants experienced time slowing down *during* the actual jump itself. A very clever second part to the study assessed this.

To try to measure whether time slowed down for the participants during the jump, the researchers made imaginative use of something called 'flicker fusion'. Imagine a red 4 on a black background. Now imagine a black 4 on a red background. Say you had a screen on which the red and black 4 are alternately displayed at a steady rate. You would see the 4 repeatedly turn from red to black to red and so on. Now imagine the alternating image display being sped up. For a while you would follow the 4 alternating between red and black, but above a certain threshold the red background of the black 4 would start to cancel out the red 4 (and vice versa) such that no digit would be discernible on the flickering display screen. In the experiment, different digits and flicker rates were used and participants were asked to name the displayed digit. The flicker speed at which each participant was just unable to identify the digit displayed was determined. For the record, this threshold was 0.047 seconds on average in the daytime, and

0.033 seconds on average at night (some of the jumps were done in the evening).

Having done all this, the volunteers had a small screen strapped to their wrist. The screen displayed red and black digits alternating at a rate that was slightly faster than their flicker threshold, which meant that under normal conditions they were unable to read the digit displayed. Then they did a second SCAD jump with the instruction that on the way down they should look at the screen and read the digits. One poor soul was unable to open her eyes to look at the screen during her jump and so she had to be excluded from the study! However, the remaining volunteers were much braver. They did manage to keep their eyes open and they were able to report which digits they believed they saw displayed during their jump.

So, the crux of the experiment is this: if time really does subjectively slow down during a life-threatening emergency, then the volunteers should experience the world in slow motion during the SCAD jump so that a display flickering too fast to read in normal conditions is slowed down and becomes readable. An ingenious piece of research – but did it work?

The answer, unfortunately, is no. Somewhat disappointingly, the volunteers were only able to report the flashing digit with around 30 per cent accuracy during the SCAD jump, which was the same level of accuracy that they managed on the ground. So it seems, then, that the feeling of time slowing down in an emergency is something one feels strongly afterwards but there was no sign that it is actually experienced during the jump itself. With only the retrospective reports showing evidence of time distortion, the study findings instead suggest that the subjective feeling of time slowing down is some kind of illusion based on recall of the event afterwards. So time doesn't actually slow down in a stressful situation – it just feels like it does. This explains why there is no 'thinking benefit' of stress that would enable parachutists to evade emergencies more effectively.

But maybe this illusion is enough. Maybe that feeling of time slowing down provides its own pleasure – its own buzz. In fact, talking of a 'buzz', perhaps this chapter has so far been missing the most important reason why you should 'stress more'. I still haven't addressed what is probably the main benefit of choosing to put yourself through the high stress of an extreme sports activity. But, thankfully, some scientists have. I can reveal that after much careful investigation, researchers have reached a fascinating conclusion – stressful activities like skydiving, SCAD jumping and bungee jumping are fun. Loads of fun in fact.

Natural high

It may seem like an obvious thing to do but researchers at the University of Hertfordshire decided to ask first-time bungee jumpers to provide ratings of the mood they were feeling at the cusp of making a jump [*see* Middleton, below]. The jumpers were questioned at the moment when, having donned the harness, they were just about to step into the safety cage. An instant later they would be winched to a height of 50 m, and once up there a staff member would yell '3- 2- 1- BUNGEE!'. And then they would be stepping out into the void to experience the rush of plummeting freefall for the few long seconds until the elastic rope would slow their descent to a full stop only to recoil them back heavenwards at similar velocity. Unsurprisingly, these first-time bungee jumpers' moods were overwhelmingly positive. In fact, feelings of positive mood increased over the hour between signing up to jump and that moment just before entering the cage. What this shows is that, despite the stress (or I suppose because of it in some strange way), doing a bungee jump is a strongly positive emotional experience.

A convincing explanation for the positive emotion experienced by bungee jumpers was found when researchers from the University of Giessen in Germany did a similar study with novice bungee jumpers, additionally collecting blood and saliva samples [*see* Hennig et al, below] Once again, doing a bungee jump was shown to produce very clear positive mood states including increased well-being, wakefulness and euphoria, not to mention decreased anxiety and sadness. But not only that – doing a bungee jump produced increased levels of the stress hormone cortisol in the saliva samples and endorphins in the blood. Cortisol is known to increase when people experience stress, so cortisol rise confirms that people experienced stress as a result of doing a bungee jump. Endorphins are best under-stood as being a morphine-like substance produced naturally by the body. Morphine is well-known to produce intense feel-ings of well-being, elation, happiness, excitement and joy, oth-erwise known as euphoria. Interestingly, among the bungee jumpers there was a correlation such that the higher the levels of endorphins, the more euphoric the jumper reported feeling. Given what we know about endorphins this correlation might well indicate that the rise in endorphin levels during a bungee jump is the cause of the euphoric feeling.

But how can stress, that negative sensation of being unable to cope with excessive demands, that scourge to health that causes deadly conditions like heart disease and depression – how can that same stress be a good thing that brings about the release of endorphins to make us feel euphoric? The answer may surprise you because contrary to what you might have heard, stress absolutely can be a good thing. In fact something I should maybe have mentioned earlier is that there are two kinds of stress known and studied by psychologists. We all know about **distress** and the negative effects it can wreak on mental and physical health. But there is another kind of stress – a positive kind known as **eustress** that people actively seek out. This opposite and pleasurable stress gains its name from the Greek *eu* (meaning 'good', as in *euphoria*) [see Selye, below].

The studies of bungee jumpers indicate how the massive stress of an extreme activity can, because it is understood as a positive experience, be perceived as the very pleasurable eustress, rather than the negative distress. And wherever there is eustress there are likely to be psychological benefits, some of which are rather surprising. Take rollercoasters, for example.

Russian mountains

Fun rides powered by gravity initially took the form of purpose-built ice hills in St Petersburg in the 17th century. The first roller coasters were giant helter-skelter slides built in Parisian parks in the early 19th century. Their resemblance to the modern-day amusement park attraction was because, instead of sliding on mats, riders sat in wheeled carts that ran on tracks. By the mid-19th century the Mauch Chunk gravity railroad in Pennsylvania, a downhill track built to deliver coal from mine to town, was being regularly opened to the paying public for pleasure rides. The first American roller coaster designed as an amusement ride, the 'Switchback Railway', opened in the 1880s at the Coney Island amusement park in New York. Interestingly, most Latin languages today know roller coasters as 'Russian Mountains', which can be traced back to the ice hills of the 17th century. What this potted history of the roller coaster demonstrates is that ever since technology has allowed it, people have been willing to pay to enjoy the eustress of a roller coaster ride.

The popularity of roller coasters is due to a combination of the enjoyment of speed (see Chapter 4) and the conquering of initial fear as well as a massive rise in physiological arousal. With regard to this latter point, fairground operators must display warning signs advising people with heart disease not to ride on roller coasters. This is for a good reason. Some cardiologists

FIGURE 6.1 Le Bon Genre/Promenades Aériennes. Onlookers watch as others use a four-storey helter-skelter with three slides

from Glasgow Royal Infirmary [*see* Pringle et al, below] measured heart rate changes in volunteers riding the *Coca Cola Roller* at the Glasgow Garden Festival in the late 1980s (later renamed *Wipeout* and moved to the Pleasurewood Hills theme park near Lowestoft, England). This 94-second ride consists of a forward and reverse run through a double corkscrew. It imparts acceleration forces of 3 g and reaches speeds of more than 40 mph. What was striking was the very large increases in heart rate it produced from a resting average of 70 beats per minute to 153 beats per minute during the ride. For some of the older volunteers this was getting uncomfortably close to what would be medically unsafe for their age. The change was all the more remarkable due to the rapidity with which the heart rate increased – all of the volunteers reached their maximum heart rate within 8 seconds of the ride starting. This level of heart-rate response is similar to that observed in parachutists and downhill skiers.

A roller coaster was the perfect stimulus for some Dutch psychologists who were interested in understanding the psychology underlying one of the most common chronic diseases of modern times [*see* Rietveld & van Beest, below]. Asthma is caused by inflammation of the small tubes, called **bronchi**, which carry air in and out of the lungs. If you have asthma, the bronchi can become inflamed and more sensitive than normal. This gives rise to the main problem facing asthmatics – **dyspnea** – the medical term for shortness of breath, coughing, wheezing and chest tightness. A windpipe that is obstructed by inflammation leads to a reduction in the amount (volume) and speed (flow) of air that can be inhaled and exhaled, known medically as **lung function**. However, there was much surprise in the 1970s when asthma researchers found that lung function and dyspnea were poorly related. In other words, some people with asthma would complain of dyspnea but have normal lung function, whereas others would show the opposite and report no dyspnea in the middle of an asthma attack.

The key to understanding this puzzle is to take into consideration the emotional state of the person with asthma at the time of asking. Specifically, it has been found that anxious individuals tend to report greater levels of dyspnea. In other words, there is a psychological dimension to asthma such that a negative emotional state leads to perception of more severe asthma symptoms. This seems to be because people with asthma learn to associate negative situations and emotional stress with difficulty in breathing. The Dutch psychologists wondered whether an opposite effect might be possible, such that rather than showing that distress leads to a greater reporting of dyspnea, what if applying eustress leads asthmatics to show reduced reporting of dyspnea because they experience a positive emotional response?

And so it was that in the name of science some asthmatic student volunteers were bussed out to a theme park in Holland and asked to ride a roller coaster – and the research findings were remarkable. While lung function, the biological measure-ment of lung efficiency, was reduced after the roller coaster ride, dyspnea, the feeling of shortness of breath, showed no resulting increase. In fact, dyspnea also reduced after the ride. What this research shows, then, is that the positive eustress of riding a roller coaster can actually reduce one of the symptoms of asthma. It shows yet another way that positive stress can be good for you. And now you are probably thinking that if posi-tive stress is so good for us, then we should all get a lot more of it. In fact, better still, what if there were a way to make bad stress good?

Turning brown eyes blue

One of the oldest ideas in psychology is the idea that feel-ing an emotion follows rather than precedes the physiological response of the body. So it's not that we see a bear, fear it and then run, but rather we see a bear, run and then we feel fear. This idea was discussed earlier on in Chapter 5 in the con-text of romantic love. If true, then all our emotional reactions are basically the same apart from how we think about them. This led psychologists from the University of Mannheim, Germany to devise a thought experiment that required vol-unteers to hold a pen in their mouth [see Strack et al, below]. Some were asked to bite its tip with the teeth, having the effect of producing a smile without the person concerned realizing it (try it and see). Others held the tip of the pen with the lips producing a pout with no trace of a smile. Pen in mouth, the volunteers were asked to rate the funniness of some Gary Larson The Far Side® cartoon drawings. Intrigu-ingly, the cartoons were rated as more funny when the pen was held with the teeth compared with the lips. This shows how smiling can improve your mood, which is contrary to the usual conception of smiling being an outward sign of the mood you are already feeling.

Taking this idea one step further, psychologists from the University of Kansas [*see* Kraft & Pressman, below] asked volunteers to bite on a pair of chopsticks, either vertically with the lips closed to produce a pout, the same but with lips apart to show the teeth in a non-committal smile, or horizontally producing a wide grin of a smile. With chopsticks in place the volunteers were then made to feel stressed. They were given the difficult task of using a pen to trace the outline of a star but they could only look at a reflection in a mirror rather than looking directly at what they were doing – making it much harder and more stressful to carry out the task without making mistakes. As if that wasn't stressful enough, they then had to submerge a hand in ice water for one minute. Both of these challenges produced a degree of stress indicated by faster heart beats. Of interest was how smiling would affect recovery from stress – and for both the star drawing task and the ice water challenge, stress recovery, in terms of how long it took for the heart beat to slow down to normal levels, was more rapid with the wide-grin smile compared with the non-committal smile or the pout.

This shows that there is something that you can do to reduce the level of distress that you feel. The old adage that one should 'grin and bear' a stressful or painful situation may be true. Grinning in the face of a challenge can reduce feelings of distress and encourage more feelings of eustress, leading to more rapid stress recovery.

Joining the EU

We have seen in this chapter that positively experienced stress, known as eustress, can be used for emotional self-regulation, can help a younger sibling establish their identity, and improve memory. It will make you feel that time has slowed down and give you the buzz of an endorphin rush. If you are asthmatic it can reduce feelings of shortness of breath. Stress is defined in our own minds so in some circumstances we can take action so that we perceive problems as challenges, converting potentially damaging negative stress into life-enhancing eustress. So it makes sense to join the EU – by which I mean try to get your share of eustress – which is something that parachutists and other extreme sport enthusiasts have known all along.

I started this chapter talking about a sociology lecturer who became a parachutist. His experiences, and the acquaintances he made during that journey, stand testament to the benefits of eustress. In fact, the research busted a stereotype about what parachutists are actually like. They're not risk junkies stopping at nothing for a thrilling dice with death. It's all about challenging yourself but few people that take up the sport intentionally increase the risk. Archetypal stories of parachutists in the 1980s taking narcotics to up the ante were alien to this community of skydivers. As one said: 'The actual danger limits... they're already there and I don't need to push them any further. I know they're there. I don't want to increase them.'

Skydivers, bungee jumpers and rollercoaster riders are looking for the spice to add to already rich and varied lives. Eustress is a guard against banality, a way of defeating the repetition that can creep into modern life. The commute, the weekend, what we eat, who we see can become dull over time. People don't have a death wish but rather the challenges of overcoming fear, of mastering new skills and just the sheer fun of high speed action are all that's needed to shake things up and make life more pleasant.

Further reading

Hardie-Bick, J. (2011), 'Skydiving and the metaphorical edge' In: Hobbs, Dick (ed.), *SAGE Benchmarks in Social Research Methods: Ethnography in context,* Vol. 3. (Sage, London, 2011)

Hennig, J., Laschefski, U., & Opper, C. (1994), 'Biopsychological changes after bungee jumping: beta-endorphin immunoreactivity as a mediator of euphoria?', *Neuropsychobiology,* Vol. 29 Issue 1 pp 28–32

Kraft, T. L. & Pressman, S. D. (2012), 'Grin and Bear It: The Influence of Manipulated Facial Expression on the Stress Response', *Psychological Science,* Vol. 23 No. 11 pp 1372–8

Leach, J. & Griffith, R. (2008), 'Restrictions in working memory capacity during parachuting: a possible cause of "no pull" fatalities', *Applied Cognitive Psychology,* Vol. 22 Issue 2 pp 147–57

Middleton, W. (1996), 'Give 'em enough rope: Perception of health and safety risks in bungee jumpers', *Journal of Social & Clinical Psychology,* Vol. 15 No. 1 pp 68–79

Pringle S. D., Macfarlane, P. W. & Cobbe, S. M. (1989), 'Response of heart rate to a roller coaster ride', *British Medical Journal,* Vol. 299 p 1575

Rietveld, S. & van Beest, I. (2006), 'Rollercoaster asthma: When positive emotional stress interferes with dyspnea perception', *Behaviour Research and Therapy,* Vol. 45 pp 977–87

Seff, M. A., Gecas, V. & Frey, J. H. (1993), 'Birth Order, Self-Concept, and Participation in Dangerous Sports, *The Journal of Psychology: Interdisciplinary and Applied,* Vol. 127 Issue 2 pp 221–32

Selye, Hans, *The Stress of Life,* Revised Edition (McGraw-Hill, New York, 1978)

Stetson C., Fiesta M. P. & Eagleman D. M. (2007), 'Does Time Really Slow Down During a Frightening Event?', *PLOS ONE* ,Vol. 2 Issue 12 e1295

Strack, F., Martin, L. L. & Stepper, S. (1988), 'Inhibiting and facilitating conditions of the human smile: A nonobtrusive test of the facial feedback hypothesis', *Journal of Personality and Social Psychology*,Vol. 54 No. 5 pp 768–77

Sulloway, F. J., & Zweigenhaft, R. L. (2010), 'Birth order and risk taking in athletics: A meta-analysis and study of major league baseball', *Personality and Social Psychology Review*,Vol. 14 No. 4 pp 402–16

Thompson, L. A., Williams, K. L., L'Esperance, P. R. & Cornelius, J. (2001), 'Context-Dependent Memory Under Stressful Conditions: The Case of Skydiving', *Human Factors*,Vol. 43 Issue 4 pp 611-19

Woodman, T., Cazenave, N. & Le Scanff, C. (2008), 'Skydiving as emotion regulation: The rise and fall of anxiety is moderated by alexithymia', *Journal of Sport & Exercise Psychology*, Vol. 30 Issue 3 pp 424–33

Yiannakis, A. (1975), 'Birth Order and Preference for Dangerous Sports Among Males', *Research Quarterly*,Vol. 47 Issue 1 pp 62–7

Yonelinas A. P., Parks C. M., Koen J. D., Jorgenson J. & Mendoza S. P. (2011), 'The effects of post-encoding stress on recognition memory: examining the impact of skydiving in young men and women', *Stress*,Vol. 14 Issue 2 pp 136–44

7
Waste time

A young man on a visit home from university sits in a garden. Spending time with his mother in the small village where he grew up is a far cry from the hustle and bustle of his Cambridge life. How dull this visit to the countryside is with little to do all day besides meandering aimlessly outside. But then again, perhaps this is valuable downtime for a busy Masters student with a good deal on his mind. Perhaps taking a break from academic life is a necessary condition to see things from a wider perspective, enabling a fuller and clearer view of the world in all its minute detail. An apple falling from a tree might, in the usual run of things, have gone unnoticed. But on this occasion a simple everyday occurrence became something of enormous significance. It reached beyond the village of Woolsthorpe-by-Colsterworth, beyond Cambridge, beyond England and, indeed, beyond planet Earth to the sun, moon and stars. Perhaps wasting time was a necessary condition for the mind of a young Sir Isaac Newton to come up with the Theory of Gravity.

This chapter explores how being an idler can have psychological benefits. From daydreaming to doodling and from chewing gum to ignoring the housework – not to mention just being plain bored – science tells us that wasting time has many hidden benefits. Indeed doing nothing can sometimes be just the thing for solving difficult problems.

Cheer up, sleepy Jean

Have you ever given up halfway through a tricky crossword but then picked it up a few hours or days later to find you could now solve clues that had previously baffled you? Sometimes what sparks going back to an abandoned puzzle is a correct answer lurching into consciousness while you were doing something else entirely. It's as though your mind was working on the solution without your realizing it. Science recognizes that people can think about problems indirectly like this and has named the process an 'incubation period'. Sometimes a tenuously connected occurrence prompts the solution – such as in Isaac Newton's case. So what is the psychology behind this incubation process?

It could be connected with the ultimate time-wasting activity of having a daydream. This was the theory of psychologists from the University of California, Santa Barbara, who have looked into this [*see* Baird et al, below]. First they had to set a problem that needed to be solved. So they asked some volunteers to suggest unusual uses for everyday objects – particularly uses beyond those the objects were designed for. So, for example, one object was a brick. Unusual uses for a brick might include utilizing it as a paperweight, as a doorstop or as a cobble in a garden path. Suggesting using it to build a wall would not count as that is its main purpose.

Next, to get their volunteers to daydream, the researchers created a deliberately boring task. It involved sitting at a computer screen on which appeared a steady stream of single-digit numbers. Most of the numbers were black but occasionally one appeared that was red or green. Volunteers were asked to respond by saying 'yes' whenever a number appeared that was both coloured AND even (i.e. a red or green 2, 4, 6 or 8). Otherwise, they had to sit quietly staring at the screen. Because most of the numbers were black they had very little to do, making it extremely difficult for the volunteers to maintain concentration. As time wore on their minds inevitably wandered so that very soon they started to do exactly what the researchers wanted – they began to daydream.

While half of the volunteers were doing the boring task the rest did a second version of the task, which was similar except slightly less boring. The volunteers still had to look out for coloured numbers but this time they were asked to respond in a different way; now they had to say whether the black number that had appeared immediately before any coloured number was even. This second version of the task required the volunteers to apply themselves a little more than the first. In this version they had to keep track and remember for a few moments every number that came on screen rather than more passively staring at the screen waiting for the coloured numbers, as required in the first task. The extra concentration needed greatly reduced the amount of daydreaming that took place.

After the volunteers had completed one or other of the computerized tasks, they were asked again to suggest unusual uses for the same objects. This enabled the researchers to see how activities during an incubation period in which a problem might be worked on unconsciously, or at least without much awareness, can affect the outcome. They found that a greater number of creative uses for objects were thought up by the volunteers who spent the incubation period doing the first boring task designed to prompt daydreaming, compared with those doing the second slightly more difficult task.

This research backs up the idea that taking a break from a difficult problem can help to solve it. Here the problem was thinking of unusual uses for objects. This is a good task to have chosen because it is so open-ended, by which I mean that there were few limits on the kinds of solution that could be suggested beyond the objects themselves. Open-endedness is also a feature of many real-world complex problems when often there is no single solution but there may be several acceptable ways to solve it. Perhaps the young Newton was daydreaming at that historic moment when the fruit detached from its branch in his mother's garden. Here is a scientific demonstration of one very useful hidden benefit of wasting time – it can help us solve difficult problems. You need never leave your sofa again!

You might have thought the story of Newton's apple was a myth, but it does appear to be true. Newton himself retold the apple story to his biographer, William Stukeley, and it appears in the book, *Memoirs of Sir Isaac Newton's Life*. However, some details I would have been interested to read about are absent. One thing that is not recorded is how tidy Newton's mother kept her garden. Believe it or not this could also have had a bearing on how history was made all those years ago.

Chores for bores

What would you rather do – tidy the house or watch TV? At work do you spend time maintaining a clean and tidy workspace or do you opt for a more laissez-faire approach? Be honest – which of the two pictures below most closely resembles your work area?

If you chose the second image then – congratulations – you are in good company. No lesser a person than Albert Einstein once reputedly said: 'If a cluttered desk is a sign of a cluttered mind, of what, then, is an empty desk a sign?' In fact, in saying this the German-born theoretical physicist, philosopher of science and developer of the general theory of relativity raised an interesting issue. Often we link physical order with morality and correctness whereas disorder is linked with immorality and deviation. But could the tidiness of your immediate environment have a bearing on how you think?

To answer this question a psychologist-lead team of marketing scientists from the University of Minnesota set up several

FIGURE 7.1 The rooms used in the orderly and disorderly conditions of Experiment 3 of the study by Kathleen D.Vohs and her colleagues

offices and meeting rooms [*see* Vohs et al, below]. Some were orderly with just a few items on desks that were neatly arranged. Others were decidedly disorderly with items strewn over surfaces and the floor, seeming as though they had been flung in a hurry rather than thoughtfully arranged. Then some volunteers were invited into the rooms and asked to carry out different tasks. In one experiment the volunteers were led to believe that a local manufacturing company was looking to diversify its markets and was trying to come up with new uses for its core product of ping-pong balls. The volunteers were asked to contribute to this by suggesting up to ten new uses for ping-pong balls. The suggestions were later rated according to how creative they were.

Fascinatingly, the volunteers in messy rooms came up with a higher number of creative uses for ping-pong balls compared with those in orderly rooms. One example of a creative use was cutting a ball in two and using each half as an ice cube tray (a considerable departure from its original intended purpose).

On the other hand, one volunteer suggested using them for 'beer pong', a drinking game in which ping-pong balls are attempted to be bounced into beer glasses (with inevitable consequences). This was viewed as low in creativity because, albeit in a different game, the item is still being used in its original sense, as a ball.

In a further experiment volunteers in messy and orderly rooms were asked to give their opinions about menus to help a local restaurateur. One set of menu items were fruit smoothie drinks with various added ingredients said to provide a boost. There was a shake portrayed as providing a 'classic health boost', and another said to provide a 'new health boost'. These menu items only differed by one word and yet, given the choice, volunteers in the orderly room more often chose 'classic' over 'new', whereas volunteers in the disorderly room did the opposite – they more often chose 'new' over 'classic'. The volunteers in the messy room were more open to novelty.

Taken together these findings indicate that orderliness aligns with a conventional mindset in which what has gone before is most prominent, whereas disorderliness prompts a more creative mindset in which novelty is valued. So, if you are stuck in a rut doing the same old things over and over again and you want to bust out of it, on the basis of this research you would be well advised to lay off the domestic chores for a while. A hidden benefit of wasting time and not bothering to tidy your home or workplace is that the resulting disorderly environment may boost your creativity and encourage you to break free from tradition and discover new things. And you get out of doing housework as well!

Let's say you decide to follow my advice and waste time by not doing anything constructive. You might find you need to find something to help pass the time – but what? Some professionals have just this dilemma because they are paid to spend hours on end sitting around doing nothing. During a game professional baseball players on the batting team have to wait patiently for their brief moments at the batter's box. If you have ever watched baseball you can't have failed to observe the two behaviours that baseball players turn to in abundance in the moments between plays: chewing and spitting. I don't intend to delve into the latter, at least not in this volume. But chewing is an interesting case – why do baseball players chew gum? A Yahoo Answers thread for just this question contained numerous replies suggesting that chewing gum helps pass the time. Certainly occupying your mouth in this way would provide a pleasant distraction. But there's more to it than this because numerous studies have shown that chewing gum has psychological benefits.

Renews vigour

Around 90 years ago when sales began to take off in North America, some people questioned whether chewing gum was an altogether suitable mass-consumer product [see Robinson, below]. Detractors considered it socially distasteful and unsightly. It's true that a certain badness of reputation still attaches itself to chewing gum. It can smack of insubordination – probably explaining why it is so loved by disaffected school pupils (and if you don't believe me have a look at the underside of any classroom desk). Indeed, Singapore banned the importing and selling of chewing gum in 1992, partly due to a spate of train delays caused by people sticking gum onto the carriage doors but also because they had a massive problem of circles of gum stuck on pavements. (The ban has since been relaxed and sugar-free gum is now widely available in Singapore.)

But it hasn't always been this way. When chewing gum was first launched as a mass consumer product in the early

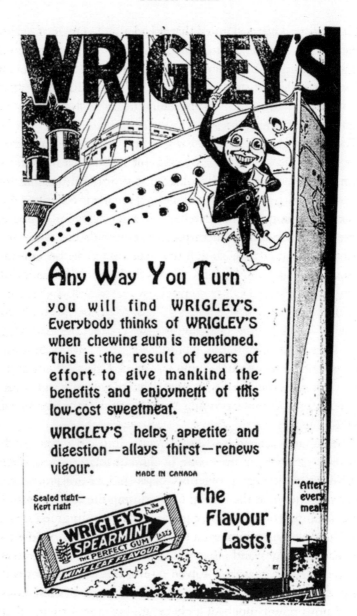

FIGURE 7.2 A 1919 newspaper advertisement for Wrigley's
Chewing Gum

20th-century adverts claimed that it had a wide range of health benefits (see picture). Gum manufacturers claimed it could relieve tension, relax the nerves and muscles, aid fatigue, quench thirst, benefit digestion and slow tooth decay. Could it be that chewing gum, the time-wasting delinquent's oral accessory of choice, is a health product?

For almost as long as gum has been on the market scientists have been on its case trying to verify (or not) the health effects claimed. Quite recently psychologists at Northumbria University in the UK [*see* Scholey et al, below] decided to test out the idea that chewing gum might relieve stress (and this was negative, unpleasant distress rather than positive, enjoyable eustress – see Chapter 6). To do this research it was necessary to devise a means of 'stressing out' some volunteers. Psychologists have codes of practice and research ethics committees that vet all studies carried out with human volunteers to ensure no harm comes to the people that take part. Waving an axe at people or torturing their relatives would, no doubt, produce a great amount of stress. However, these techniques would not make it past the committee. In this case, the volunteers were stressed out in a much less dramatic fashion: by attempting to do several computer-based tasks at the same time.

A computer screen was divided into four quadrants with four tasks going on at once, one in each quadrant. These were *arithmetic* (double-digit problems such as $16 + 17 = ?$); *distraction*, otherwise known as the Stroop task (naming the font colour of non-matching colour words, e.g. the word 'blue' in green font); *visual* (intervening whenever a moving red dot got too close to the quadrant edge); and *memory* (looking out for certain letters to appear). As soon as they solved one of the four problems it was instantly replaced by another. Doing any one of these tasks would not present much of a challenge but doing them all at the same time is enough to make anyone feel stressed, and that is exactly what the volunteers reported feeling afterwards.

The experiment itself was very simple. The volunteers completed the four-in-one task twice. One time they chewed gum as they worked, while the other time they had no chewing gum. Of interest was whether there would be differences in stress levels and task performance when the volunteers had gum compared with having no gum – and there were. When they were chewing gum the volunteers found the four-in-one task less stressful and they were more successful at it compared with when they did not chew gum. It's simple but it's scientific – these research findings support the idea that chewing gum has health benefits.

But *how* can chewing gum reduce stress? As I suggested in Chapters 5 and 6, how we experience an emotion depends on how we label it. The volunteers in the study were regular gum chewers and a number of them said they chewed gum to relieve stress. These volunteers would have noticed their heart rate increasing as they did the four-in-one task. If they believed that the heart rate increase was because of chewing (and it's well established that chewing gum raises heart rate) rather than because of the difficulty of the four-in-one task, then they would have felt less subjectively stressed, they wouldn't have been as distracted by worrying and this would have allowed them to concentrate and perform better on the four-in-one task.

However, science is a very democratic process. We would want some other scientists to repeat a similar experiment and find the same result in order to be assured that the stress-relieving properties of gum are genuine. In science this is called **replication**. Unfortunately, the stress-busting effect of chewing gum has not replicated well. A group from Coventry University [*see* Torney et al, below] found no evidence that chewing gum reduces the stress caused by trying to solve impossible anagrams (and in using such an unsolvable task simultaneously shows what a sneaky bunch psychologists can be!). A review paper carried out by scientists at Cardiff University came to the conclusion that, actually, we can't be sure yet whether chewing gum relieves stress [*see* Allen & Smith, below]. It's a standing joke among scientists that research papers often end with a statement calling for more research. This is one example of that.

Chewing gum has baggage as an unsavoury habit preferred by time-wasters. While we can't be sure yet, some research shows that chewing gum can make us feel better by reducing how stressed we feel in challenging situations. So a hidden benefit of wasting time chewing gum may be that it improves our well-being. Actually, chewing gum is not the only seemingly useless activity that can have psychological benefits – let's turn to another slacker pastime that science has recently shown to be useful.

Oodles of time

Have you ever been in a really tedious meeting or class and filled the margins of your papers with scribbles and drawings that you were barely conscious of making? Did you feel guilty at this outward display of boredom and perhaps a little unprofessional too? There might have been a good reason for doodling your way through the tedium. A psychologist from Plymouth University wondered whether doodling, a pastime usually associated with time-wasting and absent-mindedness, might actually improve performance by aiding concentration [*see* Andrade, below].

To test this idea she devised a boring experiment. Some volunteers were asked to listen to a dull telephone message from somebody organizing a party. The mock telephone message was a two-minute ramble through a series of mundane details. The volunteers were warned that the message would be dull and it didn't disappoint with gems like: 'Nigel was going to join us but he has just found out that he has to go to a meeting in

Penzance'; and: 'Suzie is going to be there too – she's the person I met at the pottery class in Harlow'. The volunteers were asked, as they listened, to write down the names of the people who definitely or probably would be going to the party, while ignoring the names of those who could not make it. So far so tedious.

While they were listening some of the volunteers were encouraged to doodle. The psychologists had to be careful how they structured this aspect of the experiment. Asking the volunteers to freeform doodle would have aroused suspicions that the drawings were going to be used as part of the experiment. This may have made the volunteers overly self-conscious making it more difficult to keep track of the message. Instead a sheet of paper containing rows of squares and circles was provided and the volunteers were asked to shade in these shapes with a pencil.

You would probably expect doodling to make it harder to keep track of what the voice on the telephone was saying. Usually doing two things at the same time is more difficult than doing just one. But in this case the opposite was true – doodling enhanced how well the volunteers were able to keep track of the partygoers' names. Doodlers, with one or two exceptions, wrote down all eight of the partygoers' names whereas most of the non-doodling volunteers missed out at least one person coming to the party. In a surprise memory test the doodlers again outperformed the non-doodlers in being able to recall more of the partygoers' names and more of the placenames mentioned in the message.

The reason why doodling made it easier to concentrate on the phone message seems to have been by reducing the tendency to 'switch off' from the message. The telephone call was deliberately boring and doodling helped maintain attention moment by moment by preventing the volunteers' minds from wandering too far. So, a hidden benefit of time-wasting by doodling is that it can help you maintain concentration and perform a dull but necessary task more effectively. Next time you are in a meeting or class and you find yourself doodling – congratulations – you were performing a conscientious act that your boss or teacher should applaud.

In this chapter so far I have talked about some of the things you may do to pass the time in avoidance of having to do something else more tedious. We have seen that daydreaming, ignoring the tidying up, chewing gum and doodling can all work in our favour. But there are times when no level of distraction can cut it. There are occasions when we find ourselves faced with a choice of things to do, none of which seem appealing. You might think that any moment spent moping about in a state of boredom like this is the epitome of wasted time and completely pointless. You'd be wrong.

The 'B' word

Imagine someone who doesn't know how it feels to be bored – how would you describe how it feels to him or her? Psychologists would explain boredom as a feeling of having no intention or purpose or being in limbo. A formal definition of boredom is having an unsuccessful desire to engage in the world [*see* Goldberg et al, below].

Actually, in real life you would be hard pushed to find someone who doesn't know how it feels to be bored. Boredom is a universal human experience – everyone finds themselves bored from time to time.

On the face of it boredom seems to serve no purpose. It disrupts the smooth flow of everyday life and when it strikes it's quite an unpleasant experience. You might wonder why boredom exists at all – and you would be in good company because many great philosophers have also paid close attention to boredom.

A recent paper by existential philosophy specialist Christian Gilliam of the University of London [*see* Gilliam, below] suggests that boredom, far from being a waste of time, actually serves a crucial purpose. But first a few words about existentialism. This branch of modern philosophy is mainly concerned with the problem of existence and the question: 'What is the meaning of life?'. For existentialists there is no clear answer to this fundamental question – and being unable to provide a satisfactory answer compels us to live in what existential philosophers have termed 'existential absurdity'. There is no meaning in the world beyond what meaning we give it – and that's where boredom comes in.

The crucial purpose of boredom, according to Gilliam, is life-affirmation, because boredom delivers the only truly authentic experience possible. How does Gilliam arrive at this conclusion? He cites Søren Kierkegaard, one of the first existential philosophers, as saying: 'Boredom rests on the nothing that interlaces existence.' When we cease to allow ourselves to be distracted by the superficiality of the world we are left with the nothing and absurdity at the core of existence – and we experience this as a feeling of profound boredom.

But this should not be viewed negatively. Getting bored compels you to try to establish a meaning. Through boredom we realize that we must create our own meaning. On the other hand, those people who do not get bored because they are immersed in the world in one way or another are viewed as superficial. Their lack of boredom marks them out as 'plebeians' in the eyes of the existential philosopher (Kierkegaard actually used this expression in this context).

So, when we have no need to do things for survival – such as to find food or to rail against oppression – we are free but we are also left in a state of existential nothingness that we experience as boredom. But painful though it is, boredom is *authentic*. The philosopher Jean-Paul Sartre compared this mindset to that of the 'Lost Boys' in *Peter Pan*. They deliberately resisted growing up and entering the bogus world of seriousness, instead staying as innocent children free to play and experience joy. By this philosophy there is a huge irony in taking life seriously because in so doing we are actually negating life.

This intriguing and easy-to-read philosophy paper argues that profound boredom is a state to be embraced rather than opposed. When you are bored you are experiencing the only true authentic experience possible. Boredom is actually a condition of possibility and opportunity. Now, these are fascinating and compelling ideas. But they are just ideas. Philosophy is a means of thinking about the world and deriving solutions via logical deduction – but you can only go so far with logic. A Sherlock Holmes needs to go into the world to verify hunches with evidence. That's where science comes in because science is our ticket to test out these philosophical ideas to see if they hold up in real life. So what does science, as opposed to philosophy, have to say about boredom?

From lectures to laundry

One way of developing a psychological understanding of a phenomenon is to collect people's personal impressions of it. A psychology study carried out at the University of New Mexico did just this [*see* Harris, below]. It recorded university student volunteers' responses to open-ended questions about boredom.

The students were asked questions such as what situations cause boredom, how they know when they are bored and whether boredom is ever positive. The top cause of boredom among university students was, ironically, lectures and classes. Next to this came having nothing to do, feeling unchallenged and monotony. The students recognized boredom by feelings of restlessness, wandering attention, feeling tired or having nothing to do. A majority of almost three-quarters said that boredom could sometimes be positive. They suggested that boredom could be an opportunity for thought or reflection, that it could be relaxing and free from stress, or could provide an opportunity to try something new or be creative.

These responses are consistent with the philosophical idea that boredom is a condition of possibility. For one thing, if we are going to accept that boredom acts to signal that a sense of meaning has been lost, then people must be able to perceive that they have become bored. Recognizing the signs of boredom was not a problem for the volunteers in the study. I should add that as a university lecturer it pains me that lectures were a number one source of boredom, although it does not altogether surprise me – I can remember disliking sitting through lectures in my own student days. Were these volunteers aware of some positive aspects of boredom? Yes – they recognized that being bored can be a trigger for self-reflection and an opportunity to try new things.

So far so good, but in some ways the study I just described has really only stated the obvious. Of course everybody knows how to recognize boredom. But if boredom really does motivate people to change what they are doing for something more meaningful then it needs to pack a significant punch. If we take awareness of pain as a similar process, for very good reason the bodily response to injury is so discomforting that it cannot be ignored. Pain directs us to take immediate action in response to a threat to our survival. The case that boredom makes us change what we are doing in order to find more meaning would be bolstered by evidence that boredom, like pain, produces physical changes in the body. But does it?

Psychologists from the University of Waterloo in Ontario [see Merrifield & Danckert, below] asked volunteers to hook up to a machine that would measure heart rate and electrodermal response (I described electrodermal response in Chapter

3) so they could measure the body's physiological responses. Next, the volunteers watched some videos chosen to put them into different moods. One video was designed to be boring; it portrayed two men hanging out washing to dry. Even though the tedium was occasionally broken when one asked the other for a spare peg (a detail that is delightfully recorded in the original research article) the volunteers all agreed that watching the four-minute film clip made them feel very bored indeed. A second video planned to invoke a neutral mood was an extract from the BBC documentary *Planet Earth* showing exotic animals and landscapes, although actually the volunteers rated this as 'interesting' rather than neutral. A third video portrayed a scene from a film in which a boy is grieving for his father's death. This was chosen to make viewers feel sad. As the volunteers watched the three films their heart rate and electrodermal response levels were constantly monitored.

Electrodermal response levels steadily decreased during all three films and were particularly low for the boring film. This reflects the tendency for the amount of attention we pay to something (in this case, a film) to reduce the longer it goes on for, and more rapidly so when it does not capture our interest. On the other hand, heart rate steadily increased throughout the boring film, but remained unchanged for the interesting and sad films. This increase in heart rate is important because it shows us that boredom is a physiologically aroused emotional state. Boredom being physiologically arousing is consistent with the philosophical idea that being bored, like pain, is a signal that we should notice and act upon. But if boredom is a state of possibility encouraging us to change our behaviour then we should be able to point to evidence that boredom alters our psychology in a way that is conducive to such a change of behaviour. So is there any evidence that boredom has psychological effects of this kind?

Turn on, tune in, zone out

The school holidays of the 1970s were, depending on how you look at it (a) a golden era of childhood when kids could be kids and wander outdoors without fear for safety; or (b) a drudge of unstructured time made all the more tedious by the absence of modern-day distractions like the Internet or multiple TV channels. In reality it was both of these, and the TV wasn't actually all that bad – at least one of the three channels available (BBC1, BBC2 and ITV) ran children's programmes in the mornings. The BBC had a show called *Why Don't You?* Its rather awkward strapline was: *Why don't you just switch off your television set and go and do something less boring instead?* Apart from illustrating that concern about overly sedentary children is not a recent thing, in reality this strapline was as unnecessary as it was unmemorable. If you leave kids in front of the TV long enough they will eventually get bored of the screen and start making their own entertainment. Evidence for this comes from research by psychologists from Pennsylvania State University.

These psychologists carried out a series of studies designed to test whether being bored makes people more creative [*see* Gasper & Middlewood, below]. The thinking was this: if boredom really does motivate us to find new activities and novel experiences then one way this would manifest itself would be a more open and creative thinking style. Similar to the last study, they got their research volunteers to watch different video clips designed to make them feel different emotions. The boring clip this time was taken from a computer screensaver programme in which an empty screen became gradually covered with differently coloured sticks.

A word game puzzle was used to measure creativity. Volunteers were supplied with three words and they had to come up with a fourth word linked to each of these three words. One example was SORE, SHOULDER and SWEAT – can you think of a word that has a link with each of these? Being able to solve puzzles like this requires a divergent thinking style. As discussed in Chapter 2, this is thinking in a far-ranging and diverse way rather than thinking in a narrow and focused way. We use this style of thinking when we are being creative. The answer to the SORE, SHOULDER, SWEAT puzzle, by the way, was COLD.

A second task to measure creativity was one where volunteers were provided with a category, such as 'vehicles' and then some example words, like 'car', 'camel' and 'tree'. They are asked to rate how well each example word fits within the category. A word like 'car' would receive a high rating because it is a good example of a vehicle. However, a word like 'camel' would receive a much more mixed rating because, clearly, it is not a vehicle, and yet it can be ridden or used to pull a cart, and so you might be tempted to rate it as being a little like a vehicle (certainly more than you would rate a 'tree' as being vehicle-like). It has been shown previously that the extent of agreement with less typical examples provides a way or measuring how creative a state of mind a person is in.

Volunteers made to feel bored solved more of the three-word problems and gave higher ratings in the category task for weak examples like 'camel'. So here is evidence that being bored really does increase levels of creativity. The findings can be explained in terms of boredom acting to motivate us to engage more in the world, and in this more motivated state we think in a more flexible way consistent with divergent rather than focused thinking. This supports the philosophical idea that boredom serves the purpose of telling us that it is time to stop what we are doing and go and do something else more meaningful.

A further direct test of the same idea was carried out by psychologists from the Universities of Michigan and Texas at El

Paso [*see* Larsen & Zarate, below]. Their research question was simple: What could people be driven to do by boredom?

1,536 arithmetic problems

Some poor unsuspecting students at the Universities of Michigan and Texas at El Paso signed up as volunteers for a study. When they arrived at the lab they were given a packet containing some simple two-digit addition and subtraction problems. This would not be a big deal were it not for the number of problems, which was more than 1,500. They were asked to sit at a desk and work through these arithmetic problems at a steady, comfortable pace, and they did this for the next 35 minutes.

Then the volunteers were lied to. They were told that due to a problem in the lab there would not now be time to do the two further experiments that had been planned. Instead, they were asked to choose which one they would do. One experiment would require them to complete some questionnaires on everyday things like eating breakfast or the place they grew up. The other experiment would require them to watch a film depicting highly negative, emotional scenes such as the aftermath of a road accident in which people had been injured. The volunteers were informed that the purpose of watching the film was to increase their physiological arousal (i.e. watching would increase their pulse rate and breathing rate) and that they would need a few minutes to calm down before leaving.

Of course, in reality there was no problem in the lab. Doing 35 minutes of arithmetic was designed to make people very bored and the second experiment they chose afterwards was a planned way to find out whether being bored actually does influence people to change their activity. The crux of the experiment was to see how being bored would influence choosing between a task that would continue the boredom by carrying on with a similar activity of filling in questionnaires, or else stop the boredom but in a way that was negative rather than positive, by watching the film. Would boredom drive people towards a distasteful activity?

The answer was 'yes'. While the number of people opting to watch the film was quite low (11 of the 48 volunteers), still there were some differences between the film watchers and the questionnaire fillers. The volunteers that wanted to watch the negatively arousing film had rated doing the maths problems as less interesting, less difficult, less pleasant and were less willing to repeat the experience compared with the volunteers who opted to carry on filling in questionnaires in the second stage. This research again supported the idea that being bored is a call to action to change what we are doing. In this case even a change towards something negative was desirable. This, incidentally, can explain some of the attraction of horror films. Even negative stimulation provoking fear and anxiety can be a suitable antidote to the boredom of everyday existence. Horror films offer just such escapism.

Boredom really can open our horizons to consider doing things that we might not otherwise do, pushing us towards wanting to experience something different even if that something is scary and challenging. There is scientific evidence for the idea that wasting time to the point of boredom can have hidden benefits. But the study I was just discussing highlighted something intriguing. Doing arithmetic problems made some people more bored than others. Why might that be, and what does it tell us about the hidden benefits of wasting time?

CD collectors

Parents – let's see if you can identify with this scenario: it is the six-week summer holidays. Your child comes to tell you

'I'm bored'. Does this happen: (a) after five weeks; (b) after one week; or (c) during the first day. If you answered anything other than (c) I would advise that you double-check whether you are, in fact, a parent. My wife tells me that when she was growing up her mum would respond to such a statement with the retort: 'only boring people get bored.' I like this. It offers a suitable chastisement for a child that needs to learn how to entertain herself. But it is built on shaky scientific foundations. It hints that boredom is something of low status that more able people can rise above. But is that really so?

Psychiatrists from Brandeis University in Massachusetts [*see* London et al, below] looked at the relationship between boredom proneness and intelligence (otherwise known as IQ). They had volunteers who, incidentally, were drawn from the military, do an extraordinarily boring task. The volunteers were asked to write the letters 'cd' over and over again for 30 minutes. They were instructed to work at a moderate pace in a relaxed and comfortable manner. It was very tedious. Certainly the volunteers rated it as more boring and less interesting than a second task of writing short stories inspired by magazine photographs. They also felt more sleepy, restless and apathetic during this very dreary half hour.

The researchers also carried out a formal IQ test with the volunteers using something called the 'Army General Classification Test' (this IQ test was developed for military use during the World Wars with the aim of improving how new recruits were assigned to suitable military roles). The researchers were interested in contrasting the volunteers' levels of intelligence with how bored they became during the 'cd' task. And there was a striking relationship. The more intelligent a person was, the more boring they found the task. In other words, the highest levels of boredom on the 'cd' task were experienced by the most intelligent among the volunteers.

While it doesn't directly contradict the idea that only boring people get bored, a parent informing their bored child that 'only intelligent people get bored' would certainly not have the desired result as a means of chastisement. Finding that intelligence is linked to boredom adds further support to the idea that boredom is a signal to stop the current activity and seek out something more meaningful. How is that so? You would expect a more intelligent person to master an activity and therefore become unchallenged more quickly than someone of lesser intelligence. If boredom acts as a signal for lack of challenge then you would expect a more intelligent person to get bored of an activity more easily, which is just what the research found. This adds yet more support to the idea that being bored, far from being a waste of time, is actually a useful and beneficial state drawing our attention to the problem that we are not using our time in a way that is conducive to our best interests.

And this is not controversial – common knowledge of the relationship between boredom and intelligence is illustrated by the everyday expression 'bored stupid'. For the last few pages I've been presenting the science that backs up the idea that boredom is a good thing. But if boredom is a good thing, and if extreme boredom is linked with stupidity, then does that make stupidity also a good thing? Most people would think wasting time being bored to the point of stupidity would be a bad move. But as we have seen there are numerous hidden benefits to being bad – and even stupidity can have its advantages.

Stupid ending

In an essay published in *The Journal of Cell Science*, microbiologist Martin Schwartz tells the story of meeting up with an old friend he had trained with at university many years before [*see* Schwartz, below]. He recalls how she had been one of the brightest people he had ever met and he had always wondered why she had gone into law after qualifying rather than do as he had done and become a scientist. Her answer came as a surprise – she had changed careers because being a scientist had made her feel stupid. She'd stuck at it for a few years but she felt stupid every day and eventually decided enough was enough. Schwartz couldn't stop thinking about what she had said until the next day it suddenly occurred to him – doing science made him feel stupid too.

He goes on to explain in the article that there is a world of difference between studying science, when you are learning about the discoveries of previous generations, to making the transition into becoming a scientist and making your own discoveries. Students do tests where there are generally 'right answers', whereas scientists have to ask themselves questions. It can often be unclear whether you are even asking the right questions let alone finding the right answers. He says that the feelings of stupidity arise because of the existential nature of life. We don't have all the answers and so we must confront our 'absolute stupidity'. Some people find that level of ignorance to be liberating. For Schwartz, faced with an almost infinite ignorance, the only course of action was to muddle through as best he could, accepting there would be mistakes along the way. Others find it deeply discouraging – and for some the step up from student to scientist is one too far because they cannot put up with regularly feeling stupid.

There are many parallels between Schwartz's short essay on scientific stupidity and how I have portrayed boredom in this chapter. I have talked about boredom as an unavoidable manifestation of our existential lives, just as Schwartz talks about our 'absolute stupidity' as an existential fact. I have talked about boredom being a call to action similar to the way that Schwartz recognizes scientific stupidity as a necessary part of the active process of scientific discovery. And while you might think that boredom and stupidity are best avoided, it seems both must be embraced in the name of progress.

So, from Sir Isaac Newton resting in his mother's garden to a self-professed 'stupid' microbiologist, this chapter has been about how wasting time can have hidden benefits. From having moments of intuition while daydreaming, to boosting your creativity by living in the mess that you have been avoiding tidying, and from chewing gum to doodling. Wasting time being bored may be the one true authentic experience open to humanity, and boredom itself stimulates action so that we stop what we are doing and switch to something more meaningful.

In fact, while you have been reading this chapter a rather large elephant has crept into the room. If wasting time is productive, then does that make being productive a waste of time? I'll leave that one for the philosophers. What I can say is this: you need never stand for anyone telling you that you are wasting time again. You have the backing of science.

Further reading

Allen, A. P. & Smith, A. P. (2011), 'A Review of the Evidence that Chewing Gum Affects Stress, Alertness and Cognition', *Journal of Behavioral and Neuroscience Research*, Vol. 9 Issue 1 pp 7-23

Andrade, J. (2010), 'What Does Doodling do?' *Applied Cognitive Psychology*, Vol. 24 Issue 1 pp 100–6

Baird, B., Smallwood, J., Mrazek, M. D., Kam, J. W. Y., Franklin, M. S. & Schooler, J. W. (2012), 'Inspired by Distraction: Mind Wandering Facilitates Creative Incubation', *Psychological Science* Vol. 23 No. 10 pp 1117–22

Gasper, K. & Middlewood, B. L. (2014), 'Approaching novel thoughts: Understanding why elation and boredom promote associative thought more than distress and relaxation', *Journal of Experimental Social Psychology*, Vol. 52 pp 50–7

Gilliam, C. R. (2013), 'Existential boredom re-examined: Boredom as authenticity and life-affirmation', *Existential Analysis*, Vol. 24 Issue 2 pp 250–62

Goldberg, Y. K., Eastwood, J. D., LaGuardia, J. & Danckert, J. (2011), 'Boredom: An Emotional Experience Distinct from Apathy, Anhedonia, or Depression', *Journal of Social & Clinical Psychology*, Vol. 30 No. 6 pp 647–66

Harris, M. B. (2000), 'Correlates and Characteristics of Boredom Proneness and Boredom', *Journal of Applied Social Psychology*, Vol. 30 Issue 3 pp 576–98

Larsen, R. J. & Zarate, M. A. (1991), 'Extending reducer/augmenter theory into the emotion domain: The role of affect in regulating stimulation level', *Personality and Individual Differences*, Vol. 12 Issue 7 pp 713–23

London, H., Schubert, D. S. P. & Washburn, D. (1972), 'Increase of autonomic arousal by boredom', *Journal of Abnormal Psychology*, Vol. 80 Issue 1 pp 29–36

Memoirs of Sir Isaac Newton's Life en.wikisource.org/wiki/Memoirs_of_Sir_Isaac_Newton%27s_life/Life_of_Newton

Merrifield, C. & Danckert, J. (2014), 'Characterizing the psychophysiological signature of boredom', *Experimental Brain Research*, Vol. 232 Issue 2 pp 481–91

Robinson, D. (2004), 'Marketing gum, making meanings: Wrigley in North America 1890–1930', *Enterprise and Society*, Vol. 5 Issue 1 pp 4-44

Scholey, A., Haskell, C., Robertson, B., Kennedy, D., Milne, A. & Wetherell, M. (2009), 'Chewing gum alleviates negative mood and reduces cortisol during acute laboratory psychological stress', *Physiology & Behavior*, Vol. 97 Issues 3-4 pp 304–12

Schwartz, M. A. (2008), 'The importance of stupidity in scientific research', *Journal of Cell Science*, Vol. 121 p 1771

Torney, L. K., Johnson, A. J. & Miles, C. (2009), 'Chewing gum and impasse-induced self-reported stress', *Appetite*, Vol. 53 Issue 3 pp 414–17

Vohs, K. D., Redden, J. P. & Rahinel, R. (2013), 'Physical Order Produces Healthy Choices, Generosity, and Conventionality, Whereas Disorder Produces Creativity', *Psychological Science*, Vol. 24 Issue 9 pp 1860-7

8

Die hard

In March 2012 the Bolton Wanderers midfielder Fabrice Muamba collapsed on the pitch during a Premier League match against Tottenham Hotspur. He had suffered a heart attack and although he was apparently dead with no vital signs for a considerable length of time, he survived. In fact, he made a rapid recovery and was discharged from hospital a month later. The only sour note in what has been a remarkable return to health was the announcement some months later of his enforced retirement from professional football, although his recent contributions as a BBC *Match of the Day* pundit have been well received.

As for the incident itself, Fabrice Muamba is on record describing his impressions of what happened. At first he felt a surreal dizziness as though he was running along inside someone else's body. The last thing he remembers is seeing two of the Tottenham player Scott Parker. Interestingly, he reports no feeling of pain as the cardiac arrest occurred and unconsciousness took hold.

I can't be the only football fan whose initial empathy for Fabrice Muamba and his family was the starting point for a deeper reflection on the episode. Obviously, it is shocking that this could happen to a fit young 23-year-old professional sports person. But beyond that, it certainly put my own mortality into sharp perspective, or more bluntly, it made me think about my future death. When will it come? (Hopefully not for many years!) What will be its circumstances? (Peaceful, I hope!). And very simply – what does it feel like to die?

Death is a fundamental issue for human beings. We are unique among all the creatures on earth in having the cognitive capacity to know that one day we will die. This means that we have to come to terms with our deaths as we go about our lives. I am not an acquaintance of Fabrice Muamba and so I can't ask him about his experiences first hand. However, as a psychologist, I do have access to the vast library of psychological research, including studies investigating the experiences of people like Muamba who have been very close to death but subsequently recovered.

The majority of such individuals have no memory of their unconsciousness although small numbers of people do recollect striking and vivid experiences. These people can recall being conscious while they were close to death and they often remember having a sense of deep calm, moving through a tunnel, meeting deceased relatives or friends, vividly and rapidly recalling major events in their lives and, sometimes, out of body experience – a feeling of floating above one's physical body and looking down at it. This constellation of memories during a period in which a person is very close to death has become known as 'near-death experience' [*see* Groth-Marnat & Summers, below].

A Frenchman visits Italy

The oldest medical description of a near-death experience was written in 1740 by a French physician called Pierre-Jean du Monchaux [*see* Charlier, below]. A Parisian apothecary who had been visiting Italy came down with a fever. At this time doctors thought that different illnesses were caused due to an excess or deficit of bodily 'humours'. The humours were blood, yellow bile, black bile and phlegm. Fever was thought to occur because of a dominance of blood and so blood-letting (withdrawing amounts of blood from the body) was believed to redress the problem and restore health.

After one bout of blood letting the apothecary reportedly suffered a syncope (pronounced sin-koh-pee) – in other words he fainted. However, he remained unconscious for long enough that the medical assistants attending to him became very worried. When the apothecary did eventually regain consciousness, du Monchaux records some extraordinary memories recalled during his brush with death. He reports: 'having lost all external sensations, he (the apothecary) saw such a pure and extreme light that he thought he was in Heaven... never of all his life had he had a nicer moment.'

This account makes it clear that a near-death experience is a very moving and powerful thing. Having the means for foreign travel in the 18th century would mean that the apothecary must have been very wealthy, yet his near-death experience apparently trumped any pleasures he may have gained from his riches, providing the nicest moment in his life. If this is really what dying feels like then it's a wonderful thing to know. If dying really is pleasant then death could be feared less and perhaps in certain circumstances even embraced.

But near-death experience is a tricky topic for science because it smacks of something spiritual, or perhaps even religious. Usually science and religion are in direct conflict (for example, consider how differently each side explains the origins of the human race). As a scientist I was sceptical about whether near-death experience is as it is claimed to be, but I was also very curious to find out more. The tale of the travelling apothecary is but one individual's story. In science we call this a case study and it falls quite low in the pecking order of what is considered to be 'good science'. A main problem here is that the story isn't verified in any way – it is just one person's word. What if the apothecary had been dreaming? Next is a more convincing account of near-death experience from the research literature – because this time a patient's version of events has been verified.

The curious case of the missing teeth

It was the night shift in a Dutch hospital and a duty nurse was one of several medical staff looking after a 44-year-old male who had been found lying in a coma [*see* van Lommel et al, below].The man was turning blue and the staff quickly decided that he needed to be put on a ventilation machine. As the nurse began feeding the air tube into the patient's mouth she found that he wore false teeth. Because these can come loose and cause problems during a medical procedure she opened his mouth and removed the dentures before carrying on hooking him up to the ventilator.The treatment seemed to be success-ful – after an hour and a half the patient's heart beat and blood pressure were returning to normal although he was still coma-tose and could not breathe unaided. He was transferred to the intensive care unit and the nurse continued working her shift.

A week later she met the patient when he was returned to the cardiac ward. The moment he saw her he said: 'Oh, that nurse knows where my dentures are.'This greatly surprised the nurse given that the patient had been in a coma when she had removed them. But he went on to say: 'Yes, you were there when I was brought into hospital and you took my dentures out of my mouth and put them onto that car, it had all these bottles on it and there was this sliding drawer underneath and there you put my teeth.'The nurse was amazed – yes, she had placed the dentures into the drawer on the trolley but how had an unconscious patient registered these details?

The man who had been in a coma went on to describe the small room in which this activity had occurred as well as the appearances of the staff that were present. He recalled having an out-of-body experience, looking down at the bustling nurses and doctors carrying out the procedure. He had been concerned that they might give up on him and he remembered desperately and unsuccessfully trying to tell the staff that he was still alive and that they should continue. The nurse corroborated this, recalling that the staff had been feeling quite negative about the patient's chances due to his poor condition upon admission to the hospital.

This is a more convincing account of an individual who had a near-death experience, all the more so because of the medical staff's corroboration. However, it is still a case study based on one person's story and there are numerous tricks and sleights of hand by which individuals with the motivation to do so can pull the wool over the eyes of onlookers. What would be yet more convincing would be studies that include more than one person's account of near-death experience.

Did you just nearly die?

One of the first attempts at a more systematic analysis of the recollections of people who had been close to death was carried out by psychiatrists based at the Universities of Michigan and Virginia at the end of the 1970s [see Greyson & Stevenson, below]. The psychiatrists corresponded with and, where possible, they interviewed members of the public who believed they had experienced the kinds of profound events while on the threshold of death that have become known as near-death experience. The events triggering these brushes with death were medical illness, traumatic injury, surgery and, in a few cases, childbirth.

Over half of the correspondents had positive experiences while close to death. Many of them experienced the well-known feeling of their life flashing before them, otherwise known as **life review**, where memories of past events appear all at once rather than in a sequence. Distortions in the perception of the passing of time were common although some correspondents felt as though time had slowed down, but others felt that time seemed to speed up. Unusual sensations were recalled such as seeing lights and auras around people, hearing noises or in some cases music, as well as feelings of warmth or absence of pain. Several perceived people to be present who could not possibly be, including people who had died years earlier. Sensations of passing through a tunnel or entering an unearthly realm were also experienced by numbers of the correspondents.

A very common element of the near-death experiences that these correspondents recalled were out-of-body experiences. As I mentioned earlier, this is the subjective sensation that you leave your body and view it from a different vantage point such as from above. The researchers collected some fascinating and very detailed accounts of these out-of-body experiences. For one thing, the process of exiting the body was said by nearly all of the correspondents to be easy to perform. It was not felt to be difficult either for the correspondents to re-enter their body at the end – this was rated as easy and instantaneous. The non-physical body they inhabited while away from their actual body was often described as being lighter in weight than their own body but the same size. Sometimes this non-physical body seemed to be without various medical conditions that they usually lived with such as deafness or missing limbs. Nearly all experienced moving about although they were never more than a few yards away from their actual body.

This research is more impressive than the earlier case studies of the apothecary and the man with the false teeth because here we have numbers of people sharing common experiences rather than isolated individual accounts. But while this study is more convincing, as science goes it's still at the 'fluffy' end of the scale; for instance, this was still very much a subjective piece of research. The study volunteers were correspondents who had answered a call for people with stories to tell to come forward. These kinds of studies run the risk that, however well meaning, the people who come forward are cranks or crave attention for one reason or another. In addition, with this type of study we can gain no idea of the prevalence of near-death experience (in other words, how likely you would be to have a near-death experience if you had a close brush with death) because we have no way of estimating the numbers of people who have brushes with death without a memorable experience. Added to these criticisms the correspondents in this study were recalling incidents that occurred anything up to six decades previously (the average was 30 years ago) and human memory being what it is these accounts may very well be unreliable. It is only comparatively recently that a more 'scientific' and objective approach has been applied to near-death experience.

A most unusual science board

A much fairer insight into the existence or otherwise of near-death experiences was provided by a study carried out around the turn of the millennium. Sam Parnia and his colleagues at Southampton General Hospital in the south of England approached all the patients in the hospital that been resuscitated following a heart attack over the course of one year [*see* Parnia et al (2001), below]. These patients could easily be identified thanks to the telephone switchboard operators who routinely logged resuscitations as they were called in through the hospital's emergency phone system. This group of individuals was ideal to form the basis of the study because cardiac arrest patients exhibit two out of the three criteria required to pronounce a person to be dead – absence of cardiac output (no heartbeat), and absence of respiratory effort (not breathing). In fact many also exhibit the third criterion of fixed dilated pupils.

The research was in three parts. In the first part, each patient was simply asked whether they had any memories from when they were unconscious following their heart attack, and if so to recount them as clearly as possible. Out of the 63 patients who underwent successful resuscitation over the 12-month study period, 7 individuals could recall their thoughts during the time they were unconscious. Four of the Southampton patients remembered coming to a point or border of no return, feelings of peace, pleasantness and joy, heightened sensual awareness and a feeling of time speeding up. These patients were classified as having had a true near-death experience because their experiences matched typical recollections recorded in previous studies. Two others remembered some details commonly encountered during near-death experience but not quite enough to be classified in the first group. The other patient recalled a less typical experience of people jumping off a mountain.

The second part of the study aimed to find out whether the body's physiological state during cardiac arrest had any bearing on the patients being able to remember their thoughts while they were unconscious. The researchers were allowed access to the patients' medical notes and these recorded the levels of oxygen, sodium and potassium in the blood during the resuscitation. To try to tease apart how these may have been affecting the patients the study drew a comparison between the four patients who were classified as having had a true near-death experience, and the 59 remaining patients in the study who did not. There was one very striking difference between the two groups – blood oxygen levels were higher in the near-death experience group of patients.

This is intriguing because one of the leading scientific theories of near-death experience at the time was that feelings such as heightened sensual awareness and time speeding up came about due to a lack of oxygen in the brain. It was thought that these phenomena occurred as the brain was starved of oxygen. The Southampton study instead suggests that rather than a lack of oxygen, it is the opposite, an availability of brain oxygen during unconsciousness that is necessary for a vivid near-death experience. There is a logic to this because better brain oxygenation would allow for improved cognitive function during the resuscitation, which would explain the more vivid experience and the ability to commit it to memory.

The third part of the study assessed out-of-body experiences in a very simple yet very clever way. The researchers had suspended special boards from the ceilings of all of the wards in the hospital. These boards had writing and figures drawn on their upper sides that would only be visible from a vantage point near the ceiling. Therefore, any participants reporting an out-of-body experience could reasonably be asked to describe what they saw on the upper sides of the boards. This would make for a very fair and very objective test of whether out-of-body experiences are real or imagined.

Suspending boards from the ceilings of all of the wards in the hospital is an astonishing amount of trouble to have gone to in order to investigate this phenomenon. But, still, it perfectly captures the true essence of what science is – using logical tests to gather evidence that will tell us something about the world that we did not know before. Science is not all about lab coats, high-tech gadgets and indecipherable equations. These investigators simply and elegantly used very low-tech painted boards to set about gathering evidence for out-of-body experiences. It's a fantastic example of what is always the core aim of scientific investigation – to carry out a fair test of the phenomenon under investigation.

Unfortunately, despite having gone to all the trouble of installing these aids, none of the seven patients with memories from their period of unconsciousness reported viewing themselves from above. Therefore, sadly, this unsophisticated but ingenious research technique was not properly put to the test. But the researchers were not finished yet. The same team of scientists with some additional colleagues carried out an updated version of the research that was published in 2014 [*see* Parnia et al (2014), below].

This was a much-improved and expanded study encompassing 15 hospitals in three different countries: the UK, the US and Austria. Once again all patients in these hospitals suffering a cardiac arrest, defined by cessation of heartbeat and breathing, and those who were successfully resuscitated were candidates to take part in the research. As before, high-level boards were installed in areas such as emergency departments and acute medical wards where resuscitations were likely to occur. These boards again had images on their top sides that would only be visible from a vantage point near the ceiling. Any resuscitated patient reporting an out-of-body experience that was able to recall the image would provide an objective verification of this unusual phenomenon.

It's not that often that when I sit reading a science paper I have a palpable feeling of anticipation but reading this paper was one of those moments. Having blogged about the Southampton study a few years previously [http://psychologyrich. blogspot.co.uk/2012/09/what-does-it-feel-like-to-die.html] I was intensely curious to find out how science would fare in this latest attempt to 'catch' in its net the ephemeral out-of-body experience.

First the details: there were 2,060 resuscitation events in all of the hospitals included in the study and 16 per cent of these were successful. This is about the going rate because, don't forget, being at the point of requiring resuscitation means that you are very ill; despite great advances in medicine the reality is that resuscitation is a last resort and most people do not survive. Many of the successfully resuscitated patients were unable to be interviewed because they were too ill or because once out of hospital they did not respond to letters sent out to them. Some, unfortunately, died before they could be contacted. Of the patients that were interviewed 9 per cent had experiences compatible with the usual definition of near-death experience. However, unlike the study a decade earlier, this time two individuals recollected vivid out-of-body experiences.

One became aware of a woman up in one corner of the room beckoning to him. He thought to himself 'I can't get up there' but he felt that she knew him and that he could trust her and, the next moment, he was up there looking down at himself and the medical staff. The memory of the experience was very vivid. He recalled hearing a voice saying: 'shock the patient, shock the patient' and he could see a nurse and a bald-headed man that he described as 'quite a chunky fella' wearing blue scrubs. The incident ended suddenly and the next thing he remembered was waking up on the bed and being told by the nurse that he had nodded off. The other resuscitation patient's recollection was more fragmented. He remembered being 'on the ceiling looking down' and seeing a nurse pumping his chest while a doctor was 'putting something down my throat'. But here's the million dollar question – could either of these two patients recall any of the images on the suspended boards?

Sorry – it's another let down. There were many hospitals in this study and it would have been unfeasible to deck out all of their rooms with boards. Only areas where resuscitations were likely to occur, such as in emergency departments and acute medical wards, were kitted out in each hospital. Unfortunately both of the patients who recalled out of body experiences underwent resuscitation in areas where it had not been possible to position boards. The research team got closer this time – closer than anyone has before – but again the opportunity to verify whether out-of-body experience is real was missed.

But, that's science. Just like in other walks of life there mostly isn't a fairy-tale ending. The researchers did go on to verify some aspects of the first patient's story in a follow-up in-depth interview (the second patient became ill and could not be interviewed again). The first patient's description of the people, sounds and activities during his resuscitation, and particularly his account of the use of an automated external defibrillator were, apparently, backed up by his medical records. But that's nothing like as convincing as a patient being able to recall the symbols and figures on the upper sides of the suspended boards would have been.

In the absence of strong evidence for near-death and out-of-body experience, there is a good deal of debate among researchers trying to explain what causes these phenomena. These lucid and sometimes spiritual occurrences are not well understood and at the moment there are two opposing views vying for supremacy.

Parascience versus science

On one side of the debate is a group [see Facco & Agrillo, below] arguing that a near-death experience, which typically may feature perceiving a tunnel, a bright light, deceased relatives, life review and sometimes out-of-body experiences, is a glimpse of the afterlife. This side considers near-death experience as paranormal, or in other words, something that conventional science cannot adequately explain. In opposition to parascience are regular scientists who believe they can explain all of the features of near-death experience in terms of psychological shock due to serious physical trauma.

Chris French, a professor of psychology at Goldsmiths, University of London provides several scientific explanations for near-death experience phenomena [see French, below]. For example, bright lights, tunnel vision, out-of-body experiences and feelings of euphoria have been reported elsewhere in the scientific literature. Fighter pilots who black out during certain high-speed manoeuvres when acceleration of their aeroplane opposes the flow of blood to the brain (known as acceleration-induced loss of consciousness, or G-LOC for short) have reported similar recollections while unconscious. G-LOC and resuscitation both involve a reduction in the usual levels of brain oxygen and both can lead to similar strange experiences.

Some other aspects of near-death experience have been seen in connection with certain physiological events. The trauma of stopped heartbeat and breathing can cause brain seizures to occur – and there are accounts of epilepsy patients reporting out-of-body experiences during seizures. Staying with electrical activity in the brain, sometimes before brain surgery a medical procedure is followed in which small electrical currents are applied to different brain regions of an awake patient in order to identify the correct area to perform surgery upon. Some of these patients have reported a 'life review' (remembering the key moments of your life rapidly and all at once), which appeared to have been triggered by the direct electrical stimulation. In addition, the generally positive tone of near-death experience can be explained by the release of endorphins as a consequence of the shock of being close to death. Endorphins are naturally occurring opioids that provide a 'high' similar to the drug heroin.

Supporters of paranormal explanations would point out that resuscitation patients have been able to recount details of their experiences while they were out cold – including the false teeth incident described earlier. However, it's possible that individuals recover consciousness at certain points during resuscitation and are able to remember what happened in those moments. Near-death experiences may occur not during full unconsciousness, but in the moments when unconsciousness sets in or as it is ending.

Out-of-body experiences can be explained in terms of their being very convincing illusions. A neuroscientist from the Department of Clinical Neuroscience at the Karolinska Institutet, Sweden, reported a fascinating study in which he was able to induce the sensation of an out-of-body experience in healthy volunteers [*see* Ehrsson, below]. He was able to make individuals feel as though they were outside their body, sitting in a chair behind the seat that their body was occupying, looking at themselves from the rear.

The illusion worked through a combination of high-tech 3D video cameras and very low-tech broom handles. Volunteers sat in a chair wearing a virtual reality-style head-mounted display. A video feed to the head-mounted display was taken from a 3D camera positioned behind the volunteer at head height for a person sitting in a chair. This would mean that although the person was sitting in one chair they would have a viewpoint as though they were sitting in another chair behind them, looking at themselves from that angle. Once settled the volunteer would be prodded gently in the chest with the blunt end of a broom handle. This was done in such a way as to not be visible, both to their camera-fed view because their body obscured the broom handle, and to their real view because the head-mounted display obscured all vision beyond the screen. At the same time, a second broom handle was moved towards a point just below the 3D camera so that the person would have seen in their display a broom handle prodding them (in effect, prodding their virtual self).

This must have been quite disorienting for the volunteer. They had visual information telling then they were situated behind their own body and then when the second broom handle was thrust towards the cameras, and hence towards their virtual self, as well as seeing it, they felt a tactile sensation of being prodded in the chest (due to the first broom handle prodding their chest out of camera shot). This all added up to a convincing illusion that they were having an out-of-body experience watching themselves from behind.

It scarcely seems ethical but the experience was ramped up a notch when the researcher later made as though to attack the virtual self with a hammer. In reality the hammer was swung below the 3D camera making it look as though it was aimed at the 'out-of-body' self. However, because they had already been brought into a state of illusion by the broom handle prodding, the volunteers showed a genuine fear response to this apparent physical attack, in the form of increased electrodermal activity (a bodily stress response – explained previously in Chapter 3). This research shows that it is possible for a person to have a very lucid feeling of being outside their own body and demonstrates that such feelings are possible, although without explaining how they may occur during near-death experiences.

One particular aspect of the phenomenon of near-death experience has been claimed as supporting both the paranormal and scientific sides of the debate. On the one hand, proponents of paranormal explanations have argued that the fact that only a small number of people who undergo successful resuscitation have a near-death experience refutes scientific explanations. They say that if near-death experiences happen due to physiological and psychological causes, then the numbers should be higher. However, those favouring conventional science explanations say the opposite. Chris French argues convincingly that people are all different such that one person may not be as affected by a certain level of reduction in brain oxygen level as another (this was shown in a study of fighter pilots affected by G-LOC). Combining these individual differences with the variation in brain oxygen levels experienced from one resuscitation to another, it seems unsurprising that there would be variability in the outcomes, so that some people have near-death experiences but others do not.

Still it is acknowledged on both sides that we don't have a full account of near-death experience using conventional scientific principles. As Chris French states, if an out-of-body experience could be verified – if it could somehow be shown that an individual did indeed have their consciousness rise up towards the ceiling above their body – then a central assumption of modern neuroscience, that consciousness is fully dependent upon the biology of the brain, would need to be rethought. There was so much riding on those suspended boards.

Yet whether or not near-death experience is a 'real' phenomenon, it could still be a compelling and life-changing experience for those 10-15 per cent of resuscitated people who experience it. In fact, researchers lead by a cardiologist at Rijnstate hospital in Arnhem carried out a study asking just this question – what happens to people in the longer term following a near-death experience? [*see* van Lommel et al, below].

From nearly dying to really living

The Dutch study was similar to the two I already discussed in that the researchers invited all patients successfully resuscitated in ten Dutch hospitals to share their experiences of surviving being clinically dead (but without the suspended boards or anything comparable). They located 344 such patients and among them 62 said that they had some recollection of the time when they were apparently lifeless. Of these, 41 had a typical near-death experience with elements such as experiencing positive emotions, feeling they were moving through a tunnel, seeing their life flash before them or meeting people that they knew to have previously died.

Two years later the researchers renewed contact with as many of these patients as they could still trace, both those who had and had not had a near-death experience. Interestingly, those who had a near-death experience seemed to have been changed by the experience. They were less afraid of death than those who had not had a near-death experience and they were more likely to believe in an afterlife. They were more interested in exploring the meaning of their life and showed more love and acceptance for others. Unusually in the world of research, which tends to take place over short timescales, the patients were contacted for a third time eight years after the initial study period. At this point the patients who had had a near-death experience still feared death to a much lesser extent than resuscitated patients that had no recollections from the time when they were unconscious and close to dying.

These long-lasting effects are remarkable given that a near-death experience lasts for only a few minutes. It seems that having a near-death experience, whether or not it is 'real', genuinely affects people, prompting them to re-evaluate their lives and attitudes. But it doesn't surprise me that this is the case. As I said at the start of the chapter, it is the unknown nature of death that contributes to its fearfulness. It seems obvious that if you had a near-death experience and especially one that is resoundingly positive, as the majority of those reported have been, it would subsequently change your attitude towards dying. What this illustrates to me is the power of psychology to change fundamental attitudes. It doesn't matter if a near-death experience is real or imagined; it would have a profound effect however it came about.

The research on near-death experience suggests that the moment of death may actually be a pleasant experience, which I take great heart from. To use the phrase in the title of this book, a hidden benefit of death is that it might not be the unpleasant experience that we assume it will be.

But science provides another good reason why death may turn out to be a more pleasant experience than expected. To explain it let me run a scenario past you. You've had a busy year. Work has been crazy and family life equally so. You have not stopped since you can't remember when and you are very much looking forward to this time next week when you will finally get to go on that foreign holiday you booked months ago. You picture the scene in your mind: there's a beach, a calm blue sea and your family members are relaxed and enjoying the weather. You lie back on your sumptuous beach towel, sip an ice cold drink and sigh in contentment…

Best Christmas ever

Of course, the daydream I've just described was bound to be too good to be true. Yes, one week later you are on a beach with your family, but getting there was a more like a military expedition than a relaxing holiday. Bags had to packed, essential items stowed and upset children needed to be consoled. When you got to the beach you realized you had forgotten the sun cream and had to retrace your steps along the 15-minute walk back to your apartment (which, incidentally, is on a somewhat busier, more urban street than you had expected). Once back at the beach you had no sooner sat down when your daughter asked to go to the shops for a fishing net. As if that wasn't enough, the refrigerator was out of order at the stall from where you got your can of coke. You take one sip of your lukewarm, sugary beverage before hauling yourself back to your feet in readiness for shopping. This is not what you had been looking forward to.

OK, so I've hammed that up a little, but it illustrates the point that things sometimes don't turn out how we think they will. Actually, I should have said 'often' instead of 'sometimes' because this mismatch between what we expect and what comes to pass is not unusual. In fact, we humans are very bad at predicting how future events will make us feel. Psychologists call this – **'affective forecasting'** – and study after study has revealed how short we fall when it comes to predicting our own futures.

One piece of research by a group at Rochester University in the US led by a psychologist was designed to compare how people thought they would react to a future event with how they

actually felt when the moment arrived [*see* Hoerger et al, below].
It all centred around some emotionally evocative pictures. Some
student volunteers first read verbal descriptions of the pictures,
for example 'a palm tree leaning out over the ocean towards the
sun as it sets' and 'police officers with nightsticks raised getting
ready to beat a homeless man on the ground'. They were first
asked to rate how they expected they would feel when looking
at these pictures on a scale running from unpleasant through to
pleasant, with several points in between. They were subsequently
shown the pictures some weeks later and this time asked to rate
how seeing each picture actually made them feel.

But how the volunteers expected to feel and how they actually felt when looking at these pictures was different – and not
always in the same way. Sometimes the volunteers felt 'more
pleasant' viewing the picture than they thought they would (this
happened in 51 per cent of the estimations), but in the other
times they felt 'less pleasant' (this happened on 49 per cent of
the estimations). It demonstrates the point that we are bad at
predicting how we will feel in future situations. Now, you could
say that this is not a fair way to research this phenomenon. Verbal
descriptions leave so much to the imagination that the volunteer would inevitably be overwhelmed or underwhelmed when
they get to see the actual picture compared with its description.
A real-world example would make for a better way of doing this
research, and such a study has been carried out.

A team led by psychologists at the University of Virginia
[*see* Wilson et al, below] looked at how happy fans of American football expected they would feel after an important college game. The match itself was between the University of
Virginia and the University of North Carolina at Chapel Hill. I
should explain for non-American readers that college football
is a much bigger deal in the US than university sport is in other
parts of the world. For example, currently the University of Virginia team, the Virginia Cavaliers, play at the 61,500 capacity

Scott Stadium located on university grounds. Now, if you think that sounds big, at the time of writing, it ranks only 27th in the list of the largest capacity college football stadia in America.

A group of students who were also football fans were asked two months before the match how they thought they would feel after the game. They were asked to rate how happy they would be if the Cavaliers lost the game, and also how happy they would be if their team won. The fans unsurprisingly expected that they would be happier if their team won, and as it happened the Cavaliers did win the game. Yet the actual level of happiness they felt the day after the match was much less than the level of happiness they had previously said they expected they would feel. Again this study demonstrates how bad we are at making accurate predictions about how future events will make us feel. I think this real-world study is more convincing than the one that involved looking at descriptions of pictures, but still, watching sports is a fairly passive activity. What about research involving some event that is lived and breathed by the people concerned?

A different team of researchers at the University of Virginia [*see* Dunn et al, below] went looking for an example of an experience that is much more fundamental to people's lives. As it turns out, a perfect scenario was right under their noses. At their university, towards the end of the first year, students are randomly allocated to the accommodation they will live in for their second, third and fourth years of college. There are 12 houses (or dormitories) overall and as well as their differing physical characteristics, they are each renowned for differing qualities such as excelling at sports, legendary parties or tolerance for minorities. This means that for different students certain houses are more desirable than others. It was traditional for students to stay up all night awaiting news of their assignment. After the announcement individuals can be seen in wild celebration or deep commiseration depending on the outcome.

This underlines how much this accommodation assignment means to the students of the University of Virginia and makes this an excellent example of something that really mattered and had a direct impact on the future lives of a group of people.

The researchers asked the students shortly before they had been assigned to a house how happy they expected to be in one year's time when they had settled in at their new dwelling. They were asked to provide a rating for how they would feel living at each of the 12 houses. One year later they were contacted again and this time asked to rate their actual happiness. Even though there was a lot more riding on this event, the findings were the same as for the picture and football studies. The students consistently overestimated how much this life event, which they judged to be very important in prospect, would affect their future happiness. The students who were assigned to houses that they considered undesirable turned out actually to be happier than they had thought they would be back in their first year (i.e. their 'actual' happiness ratings as second years were above the rating that they had assigned as first years to the house they ended up in). On the other hand, the students who were assigned to houses that were desirable were not as happy in second year as they had thought they were going to be. In fact, the actual levels of happiness of students were the same no matter whether they were assigned to desirable or undesirable houses.

What all of these studies show is that people are not good at predicting their emotional reactions to future life events. But could this extend to death? To answer this we will need to understand why we fail so miserably at forecasting our emotions. Psychologists at the University of New South Wales, Australia, have written about what underlies our inability to engage in what they describe as: 'emotional time-travel, mentally fast forwarding through time' [see Dunn & Laham, below]. One issue is that when a future event happens the psychology of that situation as it unfolds will be fundamentally different to the psychological situation that people are in when they contemplate the future event. It is difficult to imagine in prospect that we might experience death as a relief from pain and suffering but if that is so then the moment of death might be much more psychologically attractive than we would generally anticipate. The same applies to visceral factors such as pain, mood and stress, which would most likely be considerably different during the moments leading up to death than they are in those mundane moments in daily life when we might happen to think about how we will end our days.

Another reason why we predict our future emotional reactions inaccurately is because of a bias in our thinking known as 'focalism'. The holiday scenario I mentioned earlier is an example of this. We might focus on one aspect of the holiday – relaxing on a beach – forgetting the added pressure of childcare responsibilities that occur at the same time. Related to this is our tendency to think about just one relevant example rather than several. Often this will be an extreme atypical example such as the 'Best Christmas Ever' rather than all of the usual more mundane Christmas breaks we have taken. For death this bias might make us imagine a more extreme and unpleasant dramatic death such as in a car crash rather than dying in one's sleep surrounded by loved ones. A major influence preventing people from accurately predicting their future feelings is how familiar we are with the target event. For something very familiar (like a morning cup of tea) it is easy to make an accurate prediction. Death, on the other hand, is an event that we will only become familiar with through experience. This means, of course, that it is verging on the impossible to predict with accuracy the experience of death.

Although the research I have been discussing in this chapter sheds some light. The psychologists at the University of New South Wales suggest that one way of improving our ability to forecast future emotions accurately is to draw people's attention to the important features of the event that they may otherwise overlook. The near-death experience studies described in the first part of this chapter may go some way towards achieving this with respect to death given that they shed light on what may occur at the moments leading to death, and in particular the findings that these moments have been felt to be pleasant by numerous people.

This is the end

Death is usually thought of as bad but this chapter has explored whether there are hidden benefits of shuffling off this mortal coil. Fascinatingly, cardiac arrest appears not to be traumatic – of those patients that could remember the experience at all, a minority report it as unpleasant or painful. In fact where memories could be recalled they point to a joyful, peaceful experience accompanied by a pleasantly heightened sensual awareness. These findings chime with Fabrice Muamba's retelling of his experiences during a prolonged cardiac arrest on a football pitch. He said that he felt no pain whatsoever – just an odd, difficult-to-explain feeling.

So, what does it feel like to die? Given how bad we are at predicting how future events will make us feel, this is an important question to answer. On this evidence, death by cardiac arrest seems to feel either like nothing, or something pleasant and perhaps slightly mystical. Speaking to resuscitation survivors the overwhelming message is that having a cardiac arrest is not painful. We don't know if this would extend to other causes of death, but still it is reassuring. We can take comfort from the notion that death is not necessarily something to be feared. This research allows us to rest easier as we carry on our lives in death's ever present, if perhaps now slightly fainter, shadow.

Further reading

Charlier, P. (2014), 'Oldest medical description of a near death experience (NDE), France, 18th century', *Resuscitation*, Vol. 85 Issue 9 e155

Dunn, E. W. & Laham, S. A. (2006), 'A user's guide to emotional time travel: Progress on key issues in affective forecasting' In: Forgas, Joseph P. (ed.), *Hearts and minds: Affective influences on social cognition and behavior*, Frontiers of Social Psychology Series (Psychology Press, New York, 2006)

Dunn, E. W., Wilson, T. D. & Gilbert, D. T. (2003), 'Location, Location, Location: The Misprediction of Satisfaction in Housing Lotteries', *Personality and Social Psychology Bulletin*, Vol. 29 No. 11 pp 1421–32

Ehrsson, H. H. (2007), 'The Experimental Induction of Out-of-Body Experiences', *Science*, Vol. 317 No. 5841 p 1048

Facco, E. & Agrillo, C. (2012), 'Near-death experiences between science and prejudice', *Frontiers in Human Neuroscience*, Vol. 6 Art No. 209

French, C. C. (2009), 'Near-death experiences and the brain' In: Murray, Craig D. (ed.) *Psychological scientific perspectives on out-of-body and near-death experiences*, Book Series: Psychology Research Progress, pp 187–203 (Nova Science, New York, 2009)

Groth-Marnat, G. & Summers, R. (1998), 'Altered beliefs, attitudes and behaviors following near-death experiences', *Journal of Humanistic Psychology*, Vol. 38 No. 3 pp 110–125

Greyson, B. & Stevenson, I. (1980), 'The phenomenology of near death experiences', *Am J Psychiatry*, Vol. 137 Issue 10 pp 1193-6

Hoerger, M., Chapman, B. P., Epstein, R. M. & Duberstein, P. R. (2012), 'Emotional intelligence: A theoretical framework for individual differences in affective forecasting', *Emotion*, Vol. 12 Issue 4 pp 716–25

Parnia, S., Waller, D. G., Yeates, R. & Fenwick, P. (2001), 'A qualitative and quantitative study of the incidence, features and aetiology of near death experiences in cardiac arrest survivors', *Resuscitation*, Vol. 48 pp 149–56

Parnia, S., Spearpoint, K., de Vos, G., Fenwick, P., Goldberg, D., Yang, J. et al (2014), 'AWARE–AWAreness during REsuscitation–A prospective study', *Resuscitation*, Vol. 85 Issue 12 pp 1799–1805

van Lommel, P., van Wees, R., Meyers, V. & Elfferich, I. (2001), 'Near-death experience in survivors of cardiac arrest: a prospective study in the Netherlands', *The Lancet*, Vol. 358 No. 9298 pp 2039–45

Wilson, T. D., Wheatley, T., Meyers, J. M., Gilbert, D. T. & Axsom, D. (2000), 'Focalism: A source of durability bias in affective forecasting', *Journal of Personality and Social Psychology*, Vol. 78 Issue 5 pp 821–36

Other source

http://www.theguardian.com/football/2012/apr/22/fabrice-muamba-two-scott-parkers

Index